If you are not afraid of being confronted in your positions and opinions concerning the exercise of power and your relationship to civil and church authorities, this book is for you. In the tone of a prophet, the author addresses a straying Church, employing direct language and refusing to spare his reader. The theses he puts forward and the many examples he employs might disturb the citizen of the twenty-first century, but that's the point. How else can consciences be reached in such a watered-down and consensual context? His theocentric exposition is founded on the biblical texts whose language he employs. At times one would think he is reading a Reformer.

Piece by piece Berthoud dismantles the errors he discerns—and they are legion—and sheds a well-reasoned light on them. As some passages were written in the 1970s, their prophetic relevance is all the better measured half a century later. As a historian, he knows how to maintain a necessary distance from the political and ethical models particularly embraced since the beginning of the modern era. As a theologian, he vigorously traces the fabric of the spiritual warfare now at play in our world, showing the impact of a Church which ignores its responsibilities in the face of current challenges.

> **DOMINIQUE-ANTONIO TROILO,** Theologian, Historian, Pastor (Switzerland), Author of *Pierre Viret et l'anabaptisme: Un Réformé face aux dissidents protestants* and *L'oeuvre de Pierre Viret: L'activité littéraire du Réformateur mise en lumière*

---

Jean-Marc Berthoud, a prolific Swiss thinker, presents the notion of power, which is of divine origin, and how it applies to various roles in creation and culture: society, family, church and state. Difficult questions are not avoided but clearly and readably presented. Throughout, the author challenges the reader to follow the biblical notion of authority which is being globally and often violently challenged today.

> **PAUL WELLS,** Professeur émérite, Faculté Jean Calvin, Aix-en-Provence, France, Editor in chief, *Unio cum Christo*

---

All men in general, and modern Americans in particular, have an innate resentment of divine authority. Jean-Marc Berthoud faithfully upholds the heritage of the Swiss Reformers in this faithful and timely reminder that submission to the authority of God in the home, the church, and the state is not bondage. Rather, submission to the authority of God is the only way to experience true liberty.

> **JOHN HUFFMAN,** Pastor, Belleville, Illinois

---

Western civilization is reaping the antinomian and dualistic fruit of dispensationalism. This two-kingdom philosophy has led to a pacifistic and retreatist mentality that no longer engages culture but flees while waiting for the Lord to provide an escape. Churches function as corporations and businesses with pastor/elders behaving more like professionals and executives than theologians and shepherds. Little teaching is given on Biblical authority since (to conventional wisdom) this may appear insensitive, dictatorial, and lacking teamwork and cooperation. As a result, congregations, in an attempt to be accommodating, fun, and "relevant," have blurred the lines of distinction between the various institutions and have willingly embraced a different lord who promises help and safety while restricting liberty and freedom.

Thankfully, this resource is a corrective prescription to this present dearth of misunderstanding and misapplication of Scripture. This handy volume starts by defining the important source and foundation of all authority and then addresses the associated issues regarding delegated authority as expressed through its various institutions. The author then makes application of these basic principles to the many stations of life that believers encounter; be it personal responsibility, marital and family relations, ecclesiastical and governmental affairs, perspectives on the military and police, as well as an understanding of healthcare and professions.

May the Spirit grant this resource a wide readership from pastor/elders, deacons, teachers and professors, governmental magistrates and officials, as well as laity and students. This book comes at a critical time when there is much confusion on proper Biblical authority and its application. Purchase a copy for yourself and prayerfully give copies to those in your family, congregation, and community.

**STEVEN H. WOODBURY**, M.S., M.Div., Th.M., Chaplain and Teacher, Gainesville, Florida

---

How does one appeal to both reason and emotions? In our social dumbed-down media soundbite chaotic culture of no authority and (supposedly) no judgment, Jean-Marc Berthoud's *Authority in the Christian Life* cuts through the layered morass like a tear-gas cannon through an Antifa loot fest.

Memes miss the reasoning but get the emotion, while large tomes cover the reasoning and often miss the emotion; and, in these times, what topic outranks the issue of the day more so than that of *authority*? What is needed is a work that is longer than a meme while shorter than a mega-book, and *Authority in the Christian Life* delivers.

Just the table of contents alone was enough to make me want to read more: Berthoud does not hold back but covers the difference between force, authority, and power, be it in the church or the state. He doesn't shy away from the hard questions, tackling the limits of authority of both the church and the state and even spends a chapter on thinking through the question of military service.

The best part of the book for me, however, is how he exposes the socialistic revolutionary spirit of the age. Here, Berthoud is at his best, exposing the current ideological mildew to the light of scripture.

I will finish with a *may not* and a *will not*. You *may not* agree with every one of Berthoud's arguments. But you *will not* be disappointed.

**JOEL SAINT,** Pastor, Independence Reformed Bible Church, Lancaster County, PA, Executive Director of the Mid Atlantic Reformation Society

---

Jean-Marc Berthoud's *Authority in The Christian Life* trumpets a much-needed Biblical curative on the subject of authority in the Christian life, both lawful and unlawful. Not only is the theology maturely stated, but this work is also filled with instructive examples of that theology in actual circumstances. Within the Protestant world, it is almost universally conceded that all authority in heaven and earth belongs to Christ. Mr. Berthoud poses and answers a most insightful follow-up question: "Why does God delegate authority?" The answer, clearly explained, will wash away so much of the debris over this issue in our day. The glory of our magnificent God is clearly honored before the reader's mind and eyes. Tellingly, Mr. Berthoud bows before Him who is the only Sovereign with this observation: ". . . submission to the powers established by God can never be a pretext for doing the evil that these powers might order us to do or for neglecting to do the good that these powers might forbid us from doing."

May it please God to give this work a table-top reading coupled with a community-based practice in millions of homes of those who claim the name of Christ.

**TIM YARBROUGH,** Christian Business Owner & Entrepreneur, Moulton, Alabama

---

In *Authority in the Christian Life,* Jean-Marc Berthoud offers a much-needed Christological refresher course to seasoned servants of Christ and a basic primer to a new generation of disciples. For the West to be restored to her Christian foundations, and for rapidly growing churches in previously unreached people groups to become salt and light in their respective cultures, this book is a *must*. Many of the chapters speak with uncanny timeliness to today's headlines, proving once again that Gospel truth is timeless. All of them speak to the basic issues of Christian discipleship and godly nation formation. I will share this book with Christian leaders around the world who take seriously Christ's command to disciple nations. *Merci,* Jean-Marc. *Merci.*

**BISHOP WILLIAM MIKLER,** *Apostolate for the Nations*

What Jean-Marc Berthoud provides for his readers in *Authority in the Christian Life* is a breath of fresh air in the ever-growing toxic environment in Christendom. He doesn't provide a new path when thinking through submission to authority but a very old path: the path of Christian orthodoxy. In a world where many are confused about what authority we are to submit to, Berthoud provides a profound and concise answer.

**ADAM B. BURRELL**, Blogger, Author, Board member of G3 Ministries, Associate pastor of Pray's Mill Baptist Church, Douglasville, Georgia

---

During the time of the Reformation, God raised up Reformers to recover the true Gospel and to rekindle a love for God's Law. We all know their names: Martin Luther, Martin Bucer, Pierre Viret, John Calvin, Theodore Beza, and John Knox. These men established biblical principles of how Christians properly relate to the authorities of this world. Mankind, though, is forever seeking to promote independence from God's Law and all human authorities. This selfish effort only results in lawlessness, rebellion, and judgment. Now, at this time of radical social upheaval, God is raising up another spokesman, Jean-Marc Berthoud, to trumpet aloud the need for a sober reevaluation of the extent and limits of human authority. One of the most important themes of this volume, in my opinion, is its clear emphasis on how human authorities are responsible to God to be just and upright. When they are not, they fall under God's judgment and are likely to be removed by the "lesser powers." As Berthoud forcefully notes, it is not the responsibility of the individual to avenge wrongdoing—that is God's responsibility.

Thus he encourages Christians everywhere to advance the Kingdom of God on earth by utilizing spiritual weapons rather than by physical conflict. In brief, he urges Christians to not fall into the revolutionary patterns of the mob but to submit themselves to God and trust Him to make all things right. Moreover, Berthoud thoughtfully provides a number of practical scenarios to illustrate the principles he puts forward in this volume—for the businessman, the doctor or nurse, the policeman, the magistrate, the soldier, the teacher, and the church leader.

Finally, he deals with the subject of church discipline and delineates between the separated powers of the magistrate and the leaders of the church. This is biblical exposition and theological analysis at its finest. I highly recommend this volume. Read the book!

**REV. DR. MARCUS J. SERVEN**, Pastor of Christian Discipleship, Redeemer Presbyterian Church, Austin, Texas

In an age of global chaos and confusion about the rule of law, justice, and authority, theologian Jean-Marc Berthoud cuts through all the clamor to clearly explain exactly Who rules and why the topic of *Authority* is so critical to the survival of mankind. Without a proper definition of authority, which must be based upon an unchangeable absolute ethical standard of truth (i.e. the Holy Scriptures), men and nations will eventually implode, taking their place in the catalog of nations that once were, but are no more. The time has come when Christendom must exit from the shadows of their four-walled pietistic ghetto churches, removing themselves from their heretical dispensational rapture-rock, and take their place in the culture war in order to fulfill their God-given commission of cultural relevance. If Christendom fails to define culture, surely the secularists and antichrists will. The reformation and revitalization of the global order Godward is at stake. If there was ever a treatise which speaks to the tyranny that has gripped modern man, it is Berthoud's *Authority in the Christian Life*.

**DR. PAUL MICHAEL RAYMOND,** Pastor, The Reformed Bible Church in Central Virginia at Appomattox, Founder and Dean of the New Geneva Christian Leadership Academy

---

Jean-Marc Berthoud, in his short book *Authority in the Christian Life,* gives the modern Christian a true and proper Biblical understanding of the role of the civil magistrate and its relationship to the church.

What makes the book so timely in our current orchestrated crises is Berthoud's wisdom concerning the failure of civil government to exercise its authority and its complicity with evil.

His book helps restore to the church the Biblical doctrine of the role of the civil magistrate in a time of great ignorance and indifference in the church.

**THOMAS ERTL,** President, Zurich Publishing, Tallahassee

---

Through *Authority in the Christian Life,* Jean-Marc Berthoud performs a *desperately* needed and timely service for Christendom: the restoration of Biblical sanity to the conversation about legitimate authority. Between his defense of God's authority of law enforcement officials who uphold law and order over the violent, Marxist-inspired mobs in the streets of America to his prophetic call to the Church Universal to take a stand against the COVID tyrants who have run roughshod over our rights to worship, to assemble, and work, Berthoud is a living treasure.

**ADAM MCMANUS,** Anchor, *The Worldview in 5 Minutes,* a Christian newscast, heard at www.TheWorldview.com

*Everyone* interacts with some form of authority *every day*. This book gives an excellent overview of an important yet neglected subject: what the Bible says about authority. The author gives the Bible's perspective on authority in the realm of church, family, business, the military, and more. A great resource for pastors or the layperson.

**MIKE GRIGGS,** Founder, 5th Kingdom Ministries, Keystone Heights, Florida

---

Jean-Marc Berthoud's book will be a welcome read for all concerned with the overreach of government in our day and what our response should be. Power, authority, and force are carefully defined at the front of the book. God's sovereignty over His creation and institutions is an important thread woven throughout this volume with the necessary implications arising from God's rule through His Law-Word. Law and order represent God's judgment, and meaningful change, rather than arising from the destruction of God's institutions, comes by the repentance of individuals.

The Church must never give up its duty to hold forth the infallible Word in the whole counsel of God as the only hope of a stable society and the salvation of souls. Berthoud's applications are helpful to the Church as we seek to be faithful with the spiritual power given to us by Christ and to admonish the civil realm to be faithful to the power entrusted to them. "All earthly power is thus dependent on God as receiving, by delegation, a share of His power."

**MARK LIDDLE,** Pastor, Birmingham

---

Get ready for a comprehensive, practical and street level treatment of the biblical doctrine of authority. The author leaves no stones unturned. This book is a breath of fresh air in the midst of the spirit of confusion regarding authority. The confusion I am referring to exists in the Christian community toward the divinely appointed jurisdictions of the individual, of church, state, family and work. Most Christian people are very unclear regarding the authority that God has invested in these governments. Berthoud does a wonderful job unraveling the biblical truth concerning these overlapping, yet complementary and independent jurisdictions.

**SCOTT T. BROWN,** President, *Church and Family Life,* Pastor of Hope Baptist Church, Wake Forest, North Carolina

# AUTHORITY
IN THE CHRISTIAN LIFE

## BOOKS BY JEAN-MARC BERTHOUD

*Pierre Viret: the Forgotten Giant of the Reformation*

*Pierre Viret the Theologian:*
*Reformation Theology and Contemporary Application*

*Peter Ramus: Precursor to Descartes against the*
*Confessional Reformed Faith*

*In Defense of God's Law (forthcoming)*

*Calvin et la France*

*Création Bible et Science*

*Des Acts de l'Église: le Christianisme en Suisse romande*

*L'alliance de Dieu à travers l'Écriture sainte: une théologie biblique*

*L'école et la famille contre l'utopie*

*L'Église au pied du mur: Le diagnostic*
*toujours actuel du Prophète Ésaïe*

*Le Huitième Commandement:*
*L'Économie, le Vol et l'Ordre de la Création*

*Le règne terrestre de Dieu: Politique, Nations et Foi chrétienne*

*L'Histoire Alliancielle de l'Église dans le Monde*

*Une religion sans Dieu: les droits de l'Homme contre l'Évangile*

# AUTHORITY
## IN THE CHRISTIAN LIFE

by Jean-Marc Berthoud

translated by R. A. Sheats

Psalm 78 Ministries

psalm78ministries.com

*Authority in the Christian Life*

by Jean-Marc Berthoud

Translated by R. A. Sheats

Copyright © 2020 R. A. Sheats

All rights reserved.
No part of this publication may be reproduced or distributed in any form or by any means, without written consent from the publisher.

Published by:

Psalm 78 Ministries
P. O. Box 950
Monticello, FL 32345

psalm78ministries.com

ISBN: 979-8-682280124

Scripture taken from the King James Version.

# TABLE OF CONTENTS

Translator's Note . . . . . . . . . . . . . . . . . . . . . . . . . . . . . . . . . 13

Introduction by Douglas Kelly . . . . . . . . . . . . . . . . . . . . . . 15

Prologue: Two Errors to Avoid . . . . . . . . . . . . . . . . . . . . . . 21

1 All Power Comes from God . . . . . . . . . . . . . . . . . . . . . . . . . . 24

2 Power is Always Personal . . . . . . . . . . . . . . . . . . . . . . . . . . . 30

3 The Power of Mob Riots and the Disintegration of Authority . . . . . . . . . . . . . . . . . . . . . . . . . 37

4 Why God Delegates A Differentiated Form of Power to Men and Women . . . . . . . . . . . . . . . . . . . . . . . 43

5 Power, the Expression of God's Love to His Creatures . . . . 48

6 The Lawful Exercise of the Temporal Power of the Sword. . . . . . . . . . . . . . . . . . . . . . 51

7 The Limits of Christian Obedience to the Authority Ordained by God . . . . . . . . . . . . . . . . . . 56

8 Silence: Complicity with Evil . . . . . . . . . . . . . . . . . . . . . . . 61

9 Obedience to God . . . . . . . . . . . . . . . . . . . . . . . . . . . . . . . . 64

10 Contemporary Practical Examples . . . . . . . . . . . . . . . . . . 70

11  Two Types of Power:
       the Magistrate and the Church . . . . . . . . . . . . . . . . . . . . . . . 84

12  The Nature of Power within the Local Church . . . . . . . . . . . 89

13  How Can a Christian Exercise Such Power? . . . . . . . . . . . . . . 98

14  Why Does God Require Such Relationships
       of Hierarchy and Subordination? . . . . . . . . . . . . . . . . . . . . . 105

15  What Does the Necessary Separation of Powers Mean? . . . . 109

16  Conclusion . . . . . . . . . . . . . . . . . . . . . . . . . . . . . . . . . . . . . . . . 124

    Appendix: John MacArthur:
       Christ, not Caesar, is Head of the Church . . . . . . . . . . . . . 135

    Bibliography. . . . . . . . . . . . . . . . . . . . . . . . . . . . . . . . . . . . . . . . 143

# Translator's Note

—

The material that comprises this book was originally presented as lectures at the Independent Evangelical Church in Lausanne in the early summer of 1976. It was afterward published in a preliminary form in *Documentation Chrétienne* in September of 1977. The text was later revised and published as part of a larger work by Jean-Marc Berthoud entitled *Le Règne Terrestre de Dieu: du gouvernement de Notre Seigneur Jésus-Christ: Politique, Nations, Histoire et Foi chrétienne* (L'Âge d'Homme, Lausanne, 2011). In the summer of 2020, the work was slightly revised for an American audience and now appears for the first time in an English translation.

The translator wishes to express sincere gratitude to Jean-Marc Berthoud for his careful examination of the translation and his many helpful comments and corrections. May this English translation fulfill the original purpose of its author: to spread the glory of our gracious God and Savior upon a world in desperate need of the only Source of genuine truth, justice, and authority.

R. A. Sheats

# Introduction

—

The writing of Jean-Marc Berthoud is characterized both by its anchorage in the historic Christian tradition and also by its up-to-dateness, in which he engages down to the roots with modern thought, especially including its deviations from biblical reality. This work on authority does both of these things clearly and helpfully.

In doing so, he unveils what is really happening in today's most popular (as well as elite) accounts of reality. What he says on "bureaucracy"[1] and on what is "legitimate violence"[2] should be read by all who are concerned with events around us. Given the unrest in so many cities of America, his remarks on "mobs and useful idiots" illumines what is lying behind what seems to be carefully organized riots and destruction. He discusses the right of believers to resist evil[3] without at the same time seeking to bring down the entire system.[4] He shows the continuing biblical requirement of male headship[5] and gives a lucid discussion of the proper relationship between law and love.[6] His comments on the military[7] and on Christian teachers in public schools[8] are of great value to those serving in those capacities.

---

[1] page 35
[2] page 75
[3] pages 64-65
[4] page 69
[5] pages 95-97
[6] chapter five
[7] pages 74ff
[8] pages 79ff

Contrary to the generally accepted theory of "conflict of interests" in society, he demonstrates the harmony of interests at the heart of every culture.[9]

Ultimately, he takes matters down to the unseen spiritual battle that is raging over all the issues[10] and thus shows the absolute necessity of regeneration to win this battle.[11]

Douglas F. Kelly, Ph.D.

Professor Emeritus
Reformed Theological Seminary

---

[9] pages 102-104
[10] pages 98-99
[11] pages 103-104

> So will I make my holy name known in the midst of my people Israel; and I will not let them pollute my holy name any more: and the heathen shall know that I am the LORD, the Holy One in Israel.
> *Ezekiel 39:7*

There is no other will than that of God alone, which is eternal and unchanging, the rule of all justice and righteousness. He is therefore the only One we are obligated to obey without any exception. And, concerning obedience due to rulers, if they were always the mouth of God to command, it could also be said without exception that they should be obeyed as unquestionably as God. But, since the complete opposite is often the case, this condition must be established: we must obey them, provided they do not command acts of wickedness or things contrary to religion. I call *contrary to religion* the commandments by which we are commanded to do what the first table of the Law forbids or when we are forbidden to do what it commands. I call *acts of wickedness* those commands which cannot be obeyed without doing or omitting the duty that every person owes to his neighbor according to his calling, whether public or private.
Piety and love are the limits of obedience due to magistrates.
*Theodore Beza*

Power without justice is tyranny.
*Blaise Pascal*

Justice being taken away, then, what are kingdoms but great dens of thieves? For what are bands of thieves themselves except little kingdoms? The band itself is made up of men; it is ruled by the authority of a ruler. It is knit together by a social pact; the booty is divided according to the law agreed upon. If this evil is increased by the abundance of depraved men to such a degree that it maintains its own place, establishes posts of command, takes control of cities, and subjugates peoples, it more openly takes on the title of a kingdom

because the reality is now clearly conferred on it, not by the removal of greed but by the guarantee of impunity. Indeed, Alexander the Great was given a fitting reply by a pirate who fell into his hands. For, when the king asked him, "What do you mean by infesting the seas?" the man answered with frank audacity, "What you mean by seizing the entire earth! But, because I do it with a small ship, I am called a bandit. Because you do it with a great fleet, you are called Emperor!"
*St. Augustine*

For the LORD is our judge, the LORD is our lawgiver, the LORD is our king; he will save us.
*Isaiah 33:22*

In those days there was no king in Israel: every man did that which was right in his own eyes.
*Judges 21:25*

Let every soul be subject unto the higher powers. For there is no power but of God: the powers that be are ordained of God. Whosoever therefore resisteth the power, resisteth the ordinance of God: and they that resist shall receive to themselves damnation.
*Romans 13:1-2*

Submit yourselves to every *divine institution*[1] for the Lord's sake: whether it be to the king, as supreme; or unto governors, as unto them that are sent by him for the punishment of evildoers, and for the praise of them that do well.
*1 Peter 2:13-14*

---

[1] The expression *ktisis* in Greek (*creatura* in Latin) which is here translated "divine institution" literally means "creature of God," that is, an institution established by God. These are institutions whose origin is a divine creation and not merely a human invention, as the common translation generally renders it. Royalty, like any other legitimate (i.e., in accordance with the Law of God) power—such as that of the father of the family, the employer, the master, and the police officer—can only be a *creational* power of divine right. No person, in fact, and no community, has the right to arrogate power over another person. It should be noted that all rights derive their source from either God or man. We worship God only by founding our rights in Him, in His Law. Human rights, as well as any positive right based on human autonomy from God and His Law reveal the worship of man. See Jean-Marc Berthoud, *Une religion sans Dieu: Les Droits de l'Homme contre la Bible* (Messages, Lausanne, 2018).

Then Peter and the other apostles answered and said, We ought to obey God rather than men.
*Acts 5:29*

But Peter and John answered and said unto them, Whether it be right in the sight of God to hearken unto you more than unto God, judge ye.
*Acts 4:19*

# Prologue: Two Errors to Avoid

If we desire to speak justly of authority in the Christian life, there are two pitfalls that must be carefully avoided. But first we must define our terms.

We must be careful not to confuse power with authority. *Power* (*exousia* in Greek, *potestas* in Latin) is a delegation by God of His own right to man. *Authority* is the exercise of this power. We must also be careful not to confuse power and force. *Force* (*dunamis* in Greek, *potentia* in Latin) is the capacity for action, both for good or evil. Authority being the source and expression of power, power is the incarnation of authority.

Now the two pitfalls:

The first is a *challenge of the existing lawful authority,* a revolt or revolution by which men, through a carnal reaction, attempt to eliminate the "injustices" they imagine themselves to perceive.[1] In this way, they fight evil with evil and do nothing but increase evil. Such an attitude is utterly repudiated by Holy Scripture. It is indeed absurd to combat unjust *works* by employing unjust *means*.

The second pitfall we must avoid is what is called *pietism*.[2]

---

[1] The only true injustices are *violations of God's Law*. "By the law is the knowledge of sin" (Rom. 3:20).

[2] By pietism we mean a tendency (characteristic of an important part of Protestantism since the end of the seventeenth century) to limit the Christian faith to the private life of the believer. It is clear, however, that what we call "pietism" in no way sums up the Protestantism of the past three centuries. Nor is Roman Catholicism free from similar tendencies, especially in its "quietist" form. In our critique of pietism, however, we wholly dissociate ourselves from the attacks on classic Protestantism made by liberal and neo-orthodox theologians (such as Karl Barth), for their criticisms are in fact directed against the doctrine of salvation itself which these pietists still defend. Pietists are sometimes much more faithful in their practical Christian life than their doctrine would suggest. On these questions, see the developments contained in the work of E. and A. Kayayan, *Le chrétien dans la cité* (L'Âge d'Homme, Lausanne, 1995), in particular chapter three of that work: "Dualisme et vision non chrétienne dualiste du monde."

This is a view of a salvation reserved for the personal benefit of souls only and which has far too often replaced the glorious gospel of the kingdom of God. Pietism, though it rightly affirms that we must be *personally* justified, regenerated, and reconciled with God, largely forgets that the effects of this good news received by faith must extend to the entire life of the Christian, to all the thoughts and actions of the one who, in Jesus Christ, has been recreated in the image of God and through such obedience to reaching the world outside the church. For the purpose of the salvation given to the believer by pure grace is that he might produce fruit for the glory of God. These works of obedience to the Law of God manifest on earth the beginnings of His reign.

A "pietistic" attitude, confining salvation to the realm of the soul, often encourages Christians (through the effects of its antinomianism, its ignorance of the Law-Word of God) *to unreservedly and indiscriminately obey existing authorities.* Thus these Christians forget that if all power truly proceeds from God, the exercise of this power can easily become illegitimate, either by abuse or by opposition to God's order, His divine Law. When power engages in such abuses, the faithful Christian, while maintaining a respectful attitude toward these authorities, must obey God rather than men. By obeying the demands of men in such circumstances rather than those of God, unfaithful Christians recklessly surrender themselves to the disciplinary sanctions of the divine covenant. This "pietistic" error often causes, as a reaction, the opposite evil of carnal revolution against legitimate authority. We must maintain both a true submission to authority and to the primary obedience we owe to God if we are to remain in true faithfulness to the gospel of the kingdom of God. In this way the Christian will seek to *restore all things in Christ*[3] through the assistance of the Holy Spirit, in order to fulfill on earth—through faith in Jesus and obedience to His commandments—the heavenly will of the Father as it is revealed in His Law-Word.

The Greek word Paul employs in Romans 13:1 ("Let every soul *be subject* unto the higher powers") is *hupotasso*. This is a military term meaning "to place or rank under" (*hupo,* below, and *tasso,* to arrange, to order). We translate it as *submission.* Littré defines submission as "standing under authority," "recognizing authority."

---
[3] This was the motto of Cardinal Pie, bishop of Poitiers, taken up by Pope Pius X.

Littré also defines submission as "willingness to obey."

The true Christian has a supernatural willingness to obey God, for he knows that he himself is subject to the power of God. He stands under His authority, recognizes and accepts his dependence on God, and submits to the powers and authorities established by God over him, provided that these powers do not require him to disobey God and His Law.

The pagan, on the other hand, has a natural disposition to disobey both God and His Law as well as the powers that conform to the Law of God. By contrast, he will be much more willing than the faithful Christian to obey powers in rebellion against God and His Law, for he too is a rebel.

To be submissive in no way means being willing to unconditionally obey a human power.

ONE

# All Power Comes from God

God, by His very nature as Creator, possesses power and authority over all creation. Yet this power of God over His creation is not tyranny but is in essence love for His creature. For, as the only condition of man's eternal happiness, God requires us to respond to this love with repentance to God, faith in Christ and, as a result, obedience to the order willed by God and revealed in His Law-Word. Thus, all earthly power can do no more than reflect the very nature of the Almighty and Righteous God. Where this power is absent, God is not present.

However, it follows from this that, just as all power comes from God, so this power must necessarily reflect God's attributes: sovereignty, justice, effective power, wisdom, truth, goodness, love. We then understand that the text of Romans 13, where the Apostle Paul speaks of power, is not a *descriptive* text of a more or less sinful power but rather a *normative* text revealing to us God's plan in establishing, through human authorities, His power over men.[1]

**The Purpose of Power: to Uphold the Order Established by God**

The primary purpose of power is to *uphold the order established by God*. This order is not, of course, all that we call the "established order," which is usually simply a more or less sinful existing

---

[1] See Stephen C. Perks' two fundamental works, *The Nature, Government and Function of the Church: A Reassessment* (The Kuyper Foundation, Taunton, 1997) and *A Defense of the Christian State* (The Kuyper Foundation, Taunton, 1998). E. L. Hebden Taylor's books are also of tremendous help: *The Christian Philosophy of Law, Politics and the State* (The Craig Press, Nutley, 1969); *Reformation or Revolution: A Study of Modern Society in the Light of Reformational and Scriptural Pluralism* (The Craig Press, 1970); *The New Legality in the Light of the Christian Philosophy of Law* (Presbyterian and Reformed, Philadelphia, 1967); *The Reformational Understanding of Family and Marriage* (The Craig Press, 1970); *Economics, Money and Banking: Christian Principles* (The Craig Press, 1978).

order. The order that God has established and which the authorities that God has instituted have a duty to uphold is in its very nature in conformity to the divine will—that is, it corresponds to the Law of God. It is through the application of the divine order by this power of divine origin, instituted by God Himself, that God's requirements for justice for our world are revealed. Thus, by the righteous power of the sword, the wrongdoer is punished and the just person is praised.

In the end, all power possesses a necessarily spiritual character, for it is a manifestation of the sovereign power of Christ's universal grace. Through His Spirit, He sustains creation at all times and thus, in the exercise of His power, maintains "every divine institution" (1 Pet. 2:13).

This is indeed what Christ affirmed when He said, "All power is given unto me in heaven and in earth" (Matt. 28:18).

**All Power is a Reflection of God's Sovereignty**

We come now to the next point: *all power reflects the sovereignty of God.* God alone is the absolute sovereign. If a king *delegates* his authority to a governor (as the Apostle Peter says in 1 Pet. 2:14), he must recognize all the more that he himself receives this authority by the delegation of God, the Source of all authority. All earthly power is thus *dependent on God* as receiving, by delegation, a share of His power. Thus, the exercise of power is always limited by the prescriptions of *God's revealed Law.* Any power that claims to derive its origin from itself and that establishes itself as its own standard—that is, almost all modern public powers and authorities—has yielded to the original temptation of the serpent and has set itself up as its own god.

This is clearly the case of modern liberal democracy—heir of the so-called "absolute" monarchies—in which *the people* have been endowed with a sovereign power which claims to be absolute, arbitrary, and unlimited. This power decrees its own laws rather than recognizing the divine and creational origin of law and submitting its legislative control to the wholesome standards of divine Law.

The same is of course also true of so-called "totalitarian" regimes in which, in the most explicit way, *the party* becomes the sole source of power and the only standard of laws. We'll discuss this deviation later.

When a power claims autonomy and sets itself up as its own standard, it will inevitably lead to the ruin and the eradication of all freedom and human rights, as in the case of the French Revolution of 1789. On this Archbishop Marcel Lefebvre noted:

> The Decalogue comes before human rights for us, because without a Decalogue, human rights do not exist.
> The Decalogue is an objective rule—that is, one which is not contingent on the human will (either individual or collective). It is a law received with our very nature and not created by man. Here we come to the fundamental error of the Declaration of the Rights of Man of 1789, which states: "The law is the expression of the general will."[2]

Roman Catholic author Jean Madiran on his part writes:

> This Declaration claims to assert inalienable rights, but they are founded on nothing other than the general will, which could therefore modify or abolish them. This is the sin of Adam put in the plural: man claims to create his own law for himself. To the contrary, man does not create his own law; he receives it from the Creator, he finds it within his created nature. He must merely recognize and put it into practice. The function of human laws is to specify the natural law[3] in the various particular circumstances of time and place.[4]

Thus we see the final utter futility (despite their apparent temporary usefulness) of the appeals of various statesmen (or of certain oppressed Christians) to the celebrated *human rights,* founded as they are on nothing more than the supposedly general infallible will of the people themselves. This necessarily leads to basing "human rights" on man, on the worship of man, and on the religion of man.

---

[2] Statement made by Archbishop Marcel Lefebvre at Paris on May 22, 1977, recorded in *La Suisse,* May 23, 1977.

[3] Strictly speaking, this is not a *natural* law (for nature is now fallen) but rather a law of *creation,* the only infallible expression of which is located in the divine Law as revealed in the Bible. It was the fall of man and the consequent corruption of creation that made the supernatural revelation of the Law of God so necessary for mankind.

[4] Jean Madiran, "Rapport introductif sur la loi naturelle" in *Actes du Congrès de Lausanne III, Politique et loi naturelle* (C.L.C., Paris, 1967), 19.

### Power Must be Effective

The next point is this: *God's power is effective*. God invariably accomplishes what He says. Earthly power must also be effective. Where the effectiveness of power is denied or destroyed, such as in "non-correctional" teaching, "permissive" justice, or in "self-assessment" or even the so-called "participation" in the power of others, power no longer exists. Ineffective power is nothing more than the negation of power itself.

### Power has a Divine Origin

Also, Scripture teaches us that power and the institutions that stem directly from it are not primarily of *human* origin but possess a *divine* origin. Like the Law-Word of God, which gives both its form and content to every exercise of authority, power was instituted by God so that man could live and live well.

> Ye shall observe to do therefore as the LORD your God hath commanded you: ye shall not turn aside to the right hand or to the left. Ye shall walk in all the ways which the LORD your God hath commanded you, that ye may live, and that it may be well with you, and that ye may prolong your days in the land which ye shall possess. (Deut. 5:32-33)

The normative description of the exercise of power is contained in God's Law-Word, and its strength lies in the universal sustaining grace of God, that *common grace* by which Christ upholds all His creatures in order to preserve them from their innate tendency to chaos, corruption, and death, a tendency that stems from their present state of depravity. The divinely-ordained temporal power manifests its working within the framework of the institutions established by God and, in particular, by the working of justice: just punishment of the one who does evil, praise for the one who does good. It is a *wicked* thought, and one worthy of God's judgment, to affirm that institutions indispensable to the common life of men have their exclusive origin in mankind or in society, whether natural, historical, or sociological.[5] The source and purpose of these in-

---

[5] One manifestation of this error is the assertion of the thoroughly Republican Abraham Lincoln that: "No man is good enough to govern another man without that other's consent." This would mean that where there is no "full consent," there can be no power!

stitutions is found in God and in the stable order of His creation; apart from God (separated from His Law-Word), they become incomprehensible, unjustifiable, and inevitably harmful to mankind. The source, strength, and purpose of institutions are not *in man* (*humanism* or the worship of humanity), nor *in society* (*socialism*, the worship of utopian Man, which society desires to become), nor *in history* (*evolutionary historicism*, the worship of history), nor *in nature* (*pantheism*, the worship of nature), but in *God* and in *His Law-Word, a divinely established stable order manifest in creation.*[6]

## The Magistrate's Power, when Exercised According to the Righteous Law of God, is a Sign of the Power of God Himself

> And said to the judges, Take heed what ye do: for ye judge not for man, but for the LORD, who is with you in the judgment. Wherefore now let the fear of the LORD be upon you; take heed and do it: for there is no iniquity with the LORD our God, nor respect of persons, nor taking of gifts. (2 Chron. 19:6-7)

Scripture not only tells us that the judge must judge "for the Lord," but it goes even further. The presence of the judge is equivalent to the presence of God Himself. In Exodus we read about a possession left in deposit with someone and stolen by a third party:

> If the thief be not found, then the master of the house shall be brought unto the judges, to see whether he have put his hand unto his neighbour's goods. (Ex. 22:8)

Those who exercise power are indeed the servants of God. If they neglect this task, or if they perform it in a cowardly or inefficient way, they will face the judgment of their Master. One cannot assume the exercise of power without facing risks before God. John Calvin

---

Thus the authority of parents over their children; or police over criminals; or teachers over recalcitrant students, would be inherently illegitimate! This is indeed (following John Locke's theories of *consent as the foundation of power*) what the modern state claims. In this it follows the logic of its self-deification. To the contrary, what legitimizes the exercise of power isn't the "consent" of the one over whom it is exercised but rather its divine origin, its legitimacy and the conformity of its exercise to God's order.

[6] On historicism, see Joseph Siri's capital work, *Gethsemani: Réflexions sur le Mouvement Théologique Contemporain* (Tequi, Paris, 1981).

comments:

> It does not happen through the perversity of men that kings and other superiors obtain their power on earth. Rather, this comes from the providence and holy ordinance of God, who is pleased to direct the government of men in this way.[7]

---
[7] John Calvin, *Institution de la religion chrétienne* (Toulouse, 1888), 681.

TWO

# Power is Always Personal

We must next affirm that the exercise of power is always *personal,* never *collective.* The one true God, who reveals His wisdom and power in creation, who is revealed to us by Sacred Scripture and who has been incarnated in Jesus Christ, is a personal God. This God governs all His creation and the whole of history in an eminently personal way.[1]

However, since the fall of Adam and the consequent curse on the earth, *anonymous* powers[2] have been at work, tormenting creation and mankind both in their personal lives and in history (Eph. 6:12; Col. 2:8; Rom. 8:19-22). God's power over the world is personal, He who tenderly cares for the smallest bird, who knows every star by name, and who has loved men to the point of sending His own Son, Jesus Christ, as a propitiation for our sins. This power that God exercises over His creatures is neither that of a materialistic scientific determinism; nor that of the fatality of an impersonal logic; much less that of the historical necessity of the so-called laws of history. Indeed, the power that God exerts over all things is intimately personal.[3] Consequently, the power that comes from

---

[1] It is interesting to note that one of Vladimir Putin's first important actions when he became president of the Russian Federation early in 2000 was to personally sign every order he communicated to the military in Chechnya. The military, who had never witnessed such personal—and not soviet or collective—responsibility, were astounded.
[2] These are personal powers invisible to mankind—demons—but the effect of their action is impersonal, in opposition to the personal action of God and the angels. The impersonality and anonymity that often characterizes modern life is a sign of Satan's hold on our world.
[3] The God of Abraham, Isaac, and Jacob, not the abstract God of mathematics and a formal reductionist logic and reality that (wrongly!) desires to be anonymous, separated from the final ontological and epistemological authority of God and His Word as well as from the stable order of creation. See the very timely and pathbreaking work of the Anglican Thomistic philosopher, Henry Babcock Veatch (1911-1999), *Two Logics: The Conflict Between Classical and Neo-Analytic Philosophy* (Editiones Scholasticae,

God on the earthly plane must also have a personal character. The anonymous, collective, irresponsible, administrative, the consensual *group dynamic* power of corporations, committees, majorities, and bureaucracies is not the power that the Apostle Paul speaks of in Romans 13:1-7.[4]

We have seen that God delegated His power to men, who in turn can delegate this to others to bring about the order desired by the Creator on earth. In a committee, power is shared among many, which tends to render it impersonal and therefore *irresponsible*. The trinitarian God does not share His power in this way—let us repeat it, He delegates it. A shared, collective, communal power, to the extent that it tends toward irresponsibility, ceases to be a power proceeding from God.[5]

Secondly, in the Bible we never anywhere find the presence of a legitimate abstract, anonymous, impersonal power. Power is always exercised by a person, a particular judge, king, governor, officer, father, magistrate, or priest. Abstract power has become so familiar to us today (in the form, for example, of bureaucratic administration) that we no longer recognize its non-sense. An abstract power such as that of an empire, government, state, party, majority, popular sovereignty, committee, etc., hardly appears at all in the Bible other than in the symbolic form of a monstrous political *Beast* in the books of Daniel and Revelation.[6] It is well known that this symbol represents the power of the universal Empire, the lawless state, a state that has become a law to itself, a deity walking on earth, as Hegel quite rightly said of Emperor Napoleon riding through the

---

Neuenkirchen, 2019); *Intentional Logic: A Logic Based on Philosophical Realism* (Archon Books, 1970). See also the wide-ranging work of the South African Reformed Philosopher, Hendrik G. Stoker (1899-1993), *Conscience: Phenomena and Theories* (University of Notre Dame Press, Notre Dame, 2018), as well as his debate with Cornelius Van Til in E. R. Geehan, ed., *Jerusalem & Athens: Critical Discussions on the Philosophy and Apologetics of Cornelius Van Til* (Presbyterian and Reformed, Phillipsburg, 1993).

 - Ontology: part of the metaphysics that applies to being as a being
 - Epistemology: a critical study of the knowledge used to determine its logical origin

[4] On the nature of our present corporative states, see Sheldon S. Wolin, *Democracy Incorporated: Managed Democracy and the Specter of Inverted Totalitarianism* (Princeton University Press, Princeton, 2008).

[5] The Russian word *soviet* means *council* and implies collective—that is, anonymous—consensual decisions.

[6] The work of novelists such as Franz Kafka, Yevgeny Zamyatin, Aldous Huxley, Alexander Zinoviev, George Orwell, and Alexander Zinoviev, among others, admirably expresses the mind-blowing nature of this impersonal bureaucratic power.

streets of the city of Jena on his white stallion. The Bible (in Revelation 13) explicitly informs us that it is Satan himself who gives the Beast its demonic and seemingly irresistible power. This simple observation should make us reflect on the point that our civilization has reached.[7]

This does not imply a negation of the community in favor of the individual. When individuals, created in the image of God, conform themselves to God's Law, accepting their own place in His hierarchical order, community takes shape. In God's thought, "the individual" is no more opposed to the "community" than the individual divine Persons are opposed to the Trinity. It is when individuals conform their thinking and action to the precise demands of God's Law that community is created. Such a community may have powers with a collective appearance, such as the council of the Apostles in Jerusalem or the council of elders of the early churches, but here too power must be first and foremost the exercise of the personal responsibility of each individual apostle and each individual elder. It is always within the personal exercise of power by the *elders* or *apostles* (or, later, the *bishops*) that the authority of what we call a *council* manifests itself. The same is true of any power possess-

---

[7] It should be added that the just exercise of power cannot be accomplished by a centralized state. The exercise of power, the application of divine Law, is always a personal act and requires the restoration of the entire hierarchy of intermediate bodies and powers. See Michel Creuzet's book, *Les corps intermédiaires* (Montalza, 1964). I'll quote some excerpts from Olivier Delacrétaz' review article of Alexander Zinoviev's major work *Les hauteurs béantes d'Alexandre Zinoviev* (L'Âge d'Homme, Lausanne, 1977), a critical satire of bureaucratic statism, the pinnacle of which at the time was the Soviet Empire:

"A corollary thesis shows that, despite a complete stateization, private property has not been abolished but transferred to the administration—or, more precisely, the individual decision on things and people still exists, but without the weight of a corresponding responsibility, this being diffused throughout the administrative body. The overwhelming majority of the representatives of the government officially possess a tiny share of power. Hence there is a tendency to compensate for this by all means. In this, the possibilities are practically endless. Nor is it surprising that the most insignificant of public servants possesses an immense power."

Elsewhere we read:

"Ivanian power is all-powerful and, at the same time, powerless. Its omnipotence is negative—that is, it resides in its impunity to evildoing. Its impotence is positive, for it extends to its possibilities to do good without a return compensation. It possesses an immense destructive force and an insignificant creative power" (*La Nation*, Lausanne, No. 1031, July 2, 1977).

See also the chapter entitled "La technique de l'État" in the work of Jacques Ellul, *La technique ou l'enjeu du siècle* (Armand Colin, Paris, 1954).

ing a collective appearance.

**Example**

Let's consider a specific example. Scripture tells us that the father of the family has a power (delegated by God) over his entire family, including wife and children. This means that he is the one who must take ultimate responsibility before God for all that might happen under his authority within the family community. This paternal power comes from God; it belongs to him and he cannot share it with his wife, children, or servants. But his wife, too, has a power over their children that comes from God, a power for which she alone bears the responsibility before God and which she also is not able to share with her children or even with her husband. These two powers can and should *reinforce* each other, but they must not be *confused*. If the husband leaves home temporarily, he delegates his power to his wife, who then exercises a double authority, that of her husband and her own. The wife does not participate in her husband's power (which would be to "wear the pants" in the family); the husband does not participate in the power of his wife (which would be marital tyranny); children do not participate in the power of the parents (which would be a household on its head, the tyranny of children). The order desired by God must be maintained so that all members can live and thrive in the fixed framework provided by God for the happy life of the entire household. While there must not and cannot be a sharing of power between the parents, there nevertheless must be the collaboration of the two distinct powers, each coming from God, and this in a specific task—leading the family community and raising children to the glory of God. Let us insist: neither parent should abdicate their authority, nor should they encroach on or usurp the authority of the other.

We will quote some of the remarks from Alfred Kuen's excellent article, "The Christian Faced with the Crisis of Authority":

> Twenty-five years have passed since Dr. Spock published his book on the new education. In an article in *Paris-Match,* Jean Cau tells us that Dr. Spock himself had just admitted that he was wrong. Here are his words:
>
> > "It is a cruel illusion that we professionals have imposed on fathers and mothers. Certainly, we have

> acted with the best of intentions in speaking and writing about the education of children. We thought it would help them. We didn't realize until too late how much our omniscient attitude could undermine the confidence parents had in themselves.... The submission of parents to their children is not without its pitfalls. It renders them unavoidable.... Parental firmness also makes children happier."

And Jean Cau adds:

> This is a bombshell. It was America that discovered with amazement that an entire generation of youth had been placed in a mad orbit by the calculations of a deluded engineer. And who admits this? The engineer himself!

The Bible gives us principles of education: "Foolishness is bound in the heart of a child; but the rod of correction shall drive it far from him" (Prov. 22:15).

"Correct thy son, and he shall give thee rest; yea, he shall give delight unto thy soul" (Prov. 29:17; see also Heb. 12:9-11).

> Many young people say they are grateful to their parents for being tough on them. A child raised without firm authority is insecure and ultimately unhappy. The happiest children I've seen are from families in which old-style authority is practiced, but in love. I believe that if our communities do not want to experience too cruel awakenings and risk collapsing under the problems of the second generation, it is essential that parents reject the principles of education inspired by the anti-authoritarian tendencies of the period and return to the biblical principles of firmness in love.[8]

Many things cannot be delegated. We do not have the right to delegate to others what we ought to accomplish on our own. On this subject Agénor de Gasparin wrote quite rightly:

> Far too often we forget that we don't have the right—yes, the right—to fail to raise our children. Instruction is del-

---

[8] Alfred Kuen, "Le chrétien et la crise d'autorité," *Ichthus*, N° 67 (April 1977), 6-7.

egated, but education cannot be delegated. No principle that I know of requires either a father or a mother to teach all things to their children; there are many cases in which this is impracticable and many cases also, I recognize, in which this would even be undesirable. But of education, the care of the soul, and the directing of the soul, God Himself has charged them with this task.

Divine laws cannot be violated with impunity. . . . incalculable harm is caused when parents shift their burden onto the shoulders of others.[9]

**Why is Power Always Personal?**

The *raison d'être* of this inalienable personal nature of power comes from the fact that God did not create an abstraction, such as a "committee" or "bureaucracy" or "state," for He is a personal, single God, *One* in *three* Persons, and He created each of us in His image. As a result of this first fact, every person created in the image of God must, each in his own sphere, justly exercise the personal piece of power that God has given him. The notion of *participation in the power of others,* of a possible collectivization of power—a notion at the root of democracy, socialism, and communism, a notion that paradoxically ultimately leads to the "personality cult" of the totally egocentric tyrant—such a notion is an aberration, a mixture of what should remain separate, a confusion, a return to chaos.[10] This comes from sin and is nothing less than a seduction from the devil who wants to destroy the order established by God. We will be judged by God on the exercise of our personal power, and He will certainly hold us personally responsible for the abuses and crimes committed in the name of a collective power to which we have recklessly ceded our responsibilities. It will be no more possible for us to absolve ourselves of our share of responsibility for our participation in the

---

[9] Agénor de Gasparin, *La famille, ses devoirs, ses joies et ses douleurs,* Tome I (Paris, 1869), 169. See also the following excellent books: Larry Christenson, *La famille chrétienne: Foi et Victoire* (Lausanne, 1977); R. K. Campbell, *Le foyer chrétien: Bibles et traités chrétiens* (Vevey, 1976); Maurice Porot, *L'enfant et les relations familiales* (P.U.F., Paris, 1970). See also my book, Jean-Marc Berthoud, *L'école et la famille contre l'utopie* (L'Âge d'Homme, Lausanne, 1997).

[10] What is unacceptable is the claim that power comes from below, from such collective entities as humanity, the people, the party, the parliament, an oligarchy, an aristocracy, or even from a man, king, tyrant, or president. True power always comes from a personal God and is ordained by God. Everything else is no more than a reflection of man aping God—who, by doing so, surrenders himself to the devil.

exercise of a *collective* power than it was for Adam to pass the weight of his own sin onto his companion. God will not judge the works of a *committee* but rather those of each member of the committee. There is no point in doing before God what we so often do before men: hiding behind the group in whose power we *participate*—such a cowardly word!—to dodge our own personal responsibility.

THREE

# The Power of Mob Riots and the Disintegration of Authority

When individuals gather together in groups under passions of ideology, envy, or a feeling of injustice to be righted, they often become what is commonly called a "mob." Under the collective pressure of numbers, humans assembled together and frequently directed from outside often become what Vladimir Lenin used to call "useful idiots." Such mobs are easily provoked to violent action—riots—by well-trained "agents." These resolute and able revolutionaries control the ideological slogans which motivate mob violence, by which they seek to impose on society a revolutionary process so as to create, through rioting, a generalized form of social chaos from which to seize power. From this "spontaneous" violence, largely controlled from without, massed individuals are led to engage in destructive actions. Such violence is not generally desired by the majority of those individuals who take part in the originally relatively peaceful protests. This mob action, if rational from the point of view of those who direct it, is not so for those whose irrational instincts are set free from moral and legal restraints. This liberation leads to the destruction of property and, if not stopped by those in power, to the killing of innumerable human beings. Such collective mob action can sometimes take extraordinary proportions, as often seen in former revolutions.

Proverbs 24:21-22 offers the solemn warning: "My son, fear thou the Lord and the king: and meddle not with them that are given to change: for their calamity shall rise suddenly; and who knoweth the ruin of them both?"

Charles Bridges (1794-1869) writes:

Man's independence, however, naturally kicks against submission. The popular cry is for the voice and sovereignty of the people; a plain proof, that "there is no new thing under the sun" (Eccl. 1:9); since the picture of those demagogues has been drawn to the life nearly two thousand years ago—"walking after the flesh, despising government, presumptuous, self-willed, not afraid to speak evil of dignities." Such men love change for the sake of change. To become leaders of a party, they disturb the public peace by proposing changes without any promise of solid advantage. They would prefer a storm which would bring them into note, to a calm in which they were already quietly secure. They are more eager to fish for a name in troubled waters than to cultivate those quiet and social virtues which, if generally cultivated, would restrain the commotion.

"O my soul, come not thou into their secret" (Gen. 49:6). It is dangerous *to meddle with* them. . . . To be *given to change;* to undo all that has been done; to alter for the sake of altering; to be weary of the old and captivated with the new, however untried; to make experiments upon modes of government—is a fearful hazard. It is losing the substance of real good in the dream of imaginary improvements; as if we must undo everything rather than be idle. This waywardness we see in Korah's sin; in Absalom's rebellion; in the continual struggle for royalty in the Israelitish kings. How *suddenly did their calamity rise,* even when they seemed to be within the grasp of their object! *Who knoweth the ruin, which both* the Lord and the king may inflict on the despisers of their authority; often fearful beyond precedent, without remedy?[1]

Such mob action, as we have recently observed in the United States, goes hand in hand with the dissolution of authority formerly delegated by God to those established by Him to restrain public violence. However, the present humanitarian and sentimental religion so widespread in America both amongst Christians and unbelievers has now made the task of upholding law and order on the streets extremely difficult. Our societies have now largely abandoned any kind of fear of God, thereby losing the formerly commonly-held dis-

---

[1] Charles Bridges, *Proverbs* (Banner of Truth, 1968 [1846]), 456-457. Punctuation has been updated.

tinction between "good" and "evil."

This has led those in law enforcement into a terrible confusion as to the meaning of their God-given mandate: that of repressing evil and of encouraging the good. They all too often no longer clearly understand that the controlled and legitimate use of violence by the state's law enforcement agencies against all sorts of public evildoers is not only legitimate but indeed vitally necessary for the very survival of society. Such police passivity in the face of the evil actions of well-organized mobs is perhaps the most dangerous of public evils.

Another point to which we must draw our readers' attention is a very erroneous notion: that of the absolute sanctity of all human life. The true exact legal and biblical doctrine is that of the sanctity of every *innocent* human, a life which must at all costs be protected by the law. To this must be added that a certain number of actions, such as premeditated homicide, forcible rape, and the stealing of men and women in order to sell them into slavery must, according to divine law and equitable natural justice, lead to the death penalty. Whilst our society has relatively few qualms regarding the destruction of innocent human lives—as long as they are either unborn or elderly—it has great difficulty in accepting the loss of lives at the hands of the police or the military, even when this occurs in the legitimate exercise of their sacred duty to protect human lives and property and to defend the integrity of the frontiers of the nation.

That the false doctrine of the sanctity of every human life has become so great an absolute in our western civilization is due to the fact that we have forgotten that our fragile existence on earth is to be followed either by an eternity of blessedness or by unending damnation.

This, to some degree, explains why the abrogation of many of our legitimate rights (as defined by the Decalogue) through the general confinement following the outbreak of Covid-19 has met with so little opposition from all classes of society. Such tyrannical decrees leading to the imprisonment of large segments of the population of our planet thus arbitrarily placed under house arrest should have been met by the indignant, reasoned, and biblically-founded opposition of the Christian church which, in its pastors and teachers, is the ultimate God-given bulwark and pillar both of truth and justice.

**Even Misguided Powers are a Sign of Order**

Paul tells us that the existing—and consequently sinful—powers were instituted by God, and that whoever opposes them opposes the order established by God (Rom. 13:1-2). This, according to Paul, would even apply to the power of a state that has swerved from its true purpose. We must understand by such an injunction that *the very existence of misguided powers is a sign of order in relation to the absolute disorder that would exist with anarchy, chaos unleashed.* The existence of power is, therefore, as indispensable to the common life of men as the air they breathe or the water and food they consume. The air can become polluted, the water impure, and the food stale, yet their very existence allows human life to exist, though we must recognize that, in some cases, such a situation can obviously be very detrimental to the health and wellbeing of mankind. The same is true of a misguided power. For this reason, under no circumstances, even when power has become the "beast" (Rev. 13), can Christians—or any person (for Romans 13 speaks of "all souls")—claim an individual right of revolt against such a power. Order, even a wicked one, is better than the total human license to do evil.

This is not to deny that the authorities which the Reformers of the sixteenth century called "secondary powers" (the lesser magistrates) possess the right to intervene against and even suppress a harmful tyrannical power that sets itself against the common good and which would consequently be fundamentally harmful to the entire community.[2] To take an example from the mid-1970s, the Chilean army exercised such a right when it destroyed the illegal, unconstitutional, and revolutionary power of Salvador Allende and his communist supporters.

Let us simply recall the period of the absence of political power that existed during the "Liberation" of France in 1944-1945, where at least as many French were killed by other Frenchmen than were killed by the Germans throughout the entire Second World War.[3] To a certain extent, isn't it to prevent the immense political

---

[2] Douglas F. Kelly, *The Emergence of Liberty in the Modern World: The Influence of Calvin on Five Governments from the 16th Through 18th Centuries* (Presbyterian and Reformed, Philadelphia, 1992). Clémy Vautier, *Les théories relatives à la souveraineté et à la résistance chez l'auteur des "Vindiciae contra tyrannos" (1579)* (F. Roth, Lausanne, 1947).

[3] J. P. Abel, *L'âge de Caïn* (Les Éditions Nouvelles, Paris, 1947); Jean Paulhan, *Lettre*

danger that such a lack of power represents for every human community that God forbids Christians from attempting to uproot the tares from His field—the world—before the Judgment Day (Matt. 13:24-30, 36-43)? As individuals, we must respect the existing power and have a submissive attitude toward it, even when it is evil, because chaos and anarchy are even worse than organized evil. It is obvious that such an attitude of respect in no way requires obedience to evil. It should also be noted in passing that the revolt of individuals against existing authority usually only *reinforces* the systematic organization of evil, though often in another form.

We must beware of taking God's judgment into our own hands. Let us hear a text of Thomas Aquinas which admirably describes what a Christian's attitude of faith in God should be while living under an ungodly and totalitarian regime.

> "The heart of the king is in the hand of the Lord; whithersoever He will, He shall turn it" (Prov. 21:1). He turned the cruelty of the king of Assyria to pity when he meditated death to the Jews. It was He who so converted the cruel king Nabuchodonosor that he openly confessed the divine power: "Now indeed, he said, I Nabuchodonosor do praise and magnify and glorify the King of heaven because all his works are true and his ways judgments, and them that walk in pride he is able to abase" (Dan. 4:34). As for those tyrants whom He considers unworthy of conversion, He can take them from among us or reduce them to impotency, . . . Again, it is He who, seeing the affliction of His people in Egypt, and hearing their cries, cast down the tyrant Pharaoh with his whole army into the sea. Not only did He depose the proud Nabuchodonosor already mentioned, but cast him out like a beast from the company of men. Nor is His arm now any less strong to liberate His people from the oppression of tyrants. He promised His people by Isaiah to give them peace from their labors and from the confusion and dire servitude under which they once suffered. And by Ezekiel He said: "I will deliver my flock from their mouth" (34:10). That is, from those shepherds who feed only themselves. But

---

*ouverte aux directeurs de la Résistance* (Pauvert, Paris, 1968); H. Mitchell, *Les massacres de septembre 1944* (N.E.L., Paris, 1959); R. Cardinne-Petit, *Les otages de la peur* (N.E.L., Paris, 1948).

for men to merit such benefit of God they must abstain from sinning, because it is as a punishment for sin that, by divine permission, the impious are allowed to rule, as the Lord Himself warns us by Hosea: "I will give thee a king in my wrath" (13:11).[4]

---

[4] Thomas Aquinas, "De regimine principium" in *Selected Political Writings*, ed. A. P. d'Entrèves (Blackwells, Oxford, 1954), 33-35. Spelling and punctuation have been updated.

FOUR

# Why God Delegates a Differentiated Form of Power to Men and Women

All fatherhood comes from the One who is our Father in heaven (Eph. 3:14-15). Indeed, the Apostle Paul tells us in this verse that every family (*patria* in Greek) derives its name from the Heavenly Father. Thus earthly fatherhood is an "accommodated" image of the original Fatherhood, that of God.

Let us begin by remembering that though man was created in the image of God, this image and likeness is found—equally and indiscriminately—as much in women as in men. Yet let's consider what the Apostle Paul teaches to justify God's attribution of ultimate creational authority in the family (and elsewhere) to man and not woman, to man over woman and not woman over man.[1]

In his first epistle to the Corinthians, Paul tells us that Christ is the head of *every* man—Christian and unbeliever alike—and that man is the image and glory of God. This condition does not depend on man's own physical, moral, intellectual, or spiritual value but only on the fact of his being a man, a fact over which he himself still has no control. Paul adds that woman is the glory of man. (We'll look at what that means later.) Man is thus the visible earthly representative of God's power and glory. This is what we see in the account of man's creation, in which God declares that He created man in His own image and likeness (Gen. 1:27) and then created woman from man's body, a "help meet" for him, "bone of my bones, and flesh of my flesh" (Gen. 2:21-22).

Though woman was created to be the helpmeet for man, this

---

[1] Among many other books on this issue, see Stephen B. Clark, *Man and Woman in Christ: An Examination of the Roles of Men and Women in Light of Scripture and the Social Sciences* (Servant Books, Michigan, 1980); John Piper and Wayne Grudem, eds., *Recovering Biblical Manhood and Womanhood: A Response to Evangelical Feminism* (Crossway Books, Illinois, 1991).

in no way diminishes their common creation as the image of God. "So God created man in his own image, in the image of God created he him; male and female created he them" (Gen. 1:27). Together, within the above structural subordination, they share in what later came to be called the *creation mandate:*

> And God blessed them, and God said unto them, Be fruitful and multiply, and replenish the earth, and subdue it: and have dominion over the fish of the sea, and over the fowl of the air, and over every living thing that moveth upon the earth. (Gen. 1:28)

In the epistle to the Ephesians, Paul confirms what he wrote to the Corinthians. Women are required to be subject to their husbands as to the Lord Himself, for, analogically, man is the head of the woman as Christ is the head of the church (Eph. 5:22-23). And, just as the church must not assume authority over Christ but rather be subject to Him in all things, so the Apostle Paul (in his first epistle to Timothy) forbids women from assuming authority over men (1 Tim. 2:12). Peter also establishes the same relationship of authority and submission between husbands and wives (1 Pet. 3:1). Thus, in the relationship ordained by God between every man and every woman, man—*by his mere nature as a man*—symbolically (and truly) represents Jesus Christ, God. He is, as the text of the epistle to the Corinthians states, "the glory of God." And what, then, is this glory of God of which man—by God's will—should be the expression? It is nothing more than the exercise, by delegation to those placed under his responsibility, of power, of authority, of the sovereign commandment of God. Man was established by God as the delegate of His glorious power on earth.

The Apostle Paul also gives us the reasons why God thus delegated His power on earth to man. He tells us first that the man wasn't formed from the woman but the woman from the man, and that man wasn't created for woman but woman for man (1 Cor. 11:8-9; 1 Tim. 2:13). Indeed, the text of Genesis that describes the creation of woman tells us that the woman was formed from man (Gen. 2:21-22), that God made her as a help for man, a help that was suitable to him (Gen. 2:18). This text in no way states that at the beginning man was taken from woman; or that the man and woman were created at the same moment; or that the man was created to be a help for his wife; or even that the purpose of the creation of man and woman was that they should help each other in an egalitarian way. No, man was created first, then woman was taken out of man, and finally woman was given to man to be his helper. And a helper to what purpose? The power to cultivate and keep the garden, to fill the earth with human beings, and to subject the entire creation to the beneficent authority of God's Law through the power God delegated to man.[2]

God first gave to man the order to rule over the entire earth, over the fish of the seas and the birds of the air (Gen. 1:26). Then, having created man and woman, both created in His very image, He said *to the man and the woman together*: "Be fruitful, and multiply, and replenish the earth, and subdue it" (Gen. 1:28). But Paul adds still another reason to justify granting this final spiritual and creational authority to man rather than woman: Adam wasn't deceived, but Eve his wife was (1 Tim. 2:14). Confirmation of this assertion is found in the text of Genesis, where we are told that as a result of her disobedience to God, the woman's desires would be toward her husband, who would rule over her. Because of the consequences of sin, the first fully beneficent authority of man became a source of harsh domination. As long as man and woman exist, as long as heaven and earth still remain, this word of submission God addressed to the woman, to Eve, and by Eve to every woman, Christian or not, will remain.

But let us add one further remark. Though Eve sinned first, Scripture never calls the first sin the sin of Eve, but rather the sin of Adam. For, because of the fact that Adam, from his moment of creation, received by delegation the exercise of God's power, he is first of all held responsible for the sin committed by the one placed under his failing and deficient authority. For he was ordered by God to keep or guard the garden and cultivate it, and he failed in the exercise of this responsibility. Where God grants greater authority and power, He also demands more responsibility (Heb. 13:17; Jas. 3:1).

---

[2] On the confusion between the beneficent creation mandate of Genesis and the pretensions of industrial and technological modernity to exploit and dominate creation for the sole egotistical material interest of man (as formulated both by Francis Bacon and René Descartes), see the pioneering work of Cameron Wybrow, *The Bible, Baconianism, and Mastery over Nature: The Old Testament and its Modern Misreading* (Peter Lang, Bern, 1991).

If man is the glory of God, if he is the image of God Himself, what then is woman? Paul tells us that the woman, in her own right an image of God, is the glory of man. We must now ask: what then is the glory of man in the face of his Creator? It is that glory which comes from his obedience, from his submission to God, from the fact that he obeys Him. Man was created by God to glorify and obey Him in all things. If Adam—and, in him, both man and woman—were created in the image and likeness of God (Gen. 1:26-27), woman, on the other hand, was created in the likeness of man (Gen. 2:18) with the purpose of being his help meet. In this she represents all men before God, men created by Him to glorify Him and to obey Him. Thus, within the created world, man represents God and the woman represents man, and the earthly man-woman relationship of husband-wife represents the God-creature relationship of Christ and the church, the concord between the Creator and His creation. This is the reason why He demands the woman to submit to her husband as to the Lord (Eph. 5:22) just as the church is submitted to her head, Jesus Christ. For, let us always remember, man here on earth represents the Lord God Himself.

This in no way implies an inferiority of women vis-à-vis man or even a complementarity between them,[3] but a blessed relationship of both hierarchical authority and mutual submission between men and women. The authority of man over woman is thus a figure of God's sovereign authority over mankind and over His church and of the submission of mankind to their Creator and of the church to its head, Jesus Christ. By maintaining his God-given power, his authority over woman, man publicly witnesses to God's sovereignty over His creation and to Christ's over His church. In accepting this submission to man, woman also—through her practice of the Truth—publicly witnesses to the submission of the creature to the Creator and of the church to Christ. It is by each person fulfilling the place assigned to them by God in the family, in society, and in the church that men and women uphold the fundamental order between God and His creatures.

This principle of the primacy of male authority and responsibility before God being firmly established as a part of the order

---

[3] The notion of complementarianism extends far beyond the couple to find full expression in the church, the body of Christ. Here we are merely examining that aspect which relates to the family.

of creation reflecting God's relation to His creatures, we must add that this includes for both men and women differentiated spheres of responsibility that do not give men any kind of overweening and tyrannical power over women in the specific fields of their activities. This limitation applies to every kind of creational hierarchy (Eph. 6:5-9). In the Trinity, the Father has primacy with regard to the Son, but this does not imply subservience of the Son to the Father. The authority which belongs to the Son, however, is not in any way in competition with that exercised in the unity of the Trinity by the Father or the Holy Spirit. Thus, according to their specific natures—male or female—and to their particular vocations, both men and women have a degree of harmonious autonomous responsibility, one with regard to the other, in their specific fields of activity, whether it be in his study for man or in the household for woman. But this diversity in unity in no way contradicts the ultimate authority and responsibility, before God, of man over woman, of the husband over the wife. The source, to take but one example, of feminism is not first to be sought in the revolt of the woman but in the refusal by men—for reasons of their own convenience—to exercise that difficult authority so intimately bound to their fundamental responsibility.

By ceding his creational place to the woman in the family, in society, and in the church, man, before the eyes of all creation, subjects God to the creature and Christ to the church. By taking man's place in the family, in society, or in the church, woman actually attempts to subjugate God to the creature and Christ to the church. The woman's desire to dominate over man is nothing more than man and the church's desire (inspired here by Satan) to place themselves above God, to rule over God, to make themselves equal with God (Gen. 3:5).

Thus, by each person, male and female, maintaining the place given to them by God in creation—even in the outward signs of hair and clothing—man and woman testify to the foundation of all order on earth, testifying to the glory of God and to God's absolute and beneficent sovereignty over His creatures. They publicly reveal this glory of man, which is nothing more than obedience and submission to God so that men can live and exercise a beneficent dominion over creation by submitting it to God. This is how God's will is done on earth as it is in heaven. This is how the blessed kingdom of God and His Christ is extended throughout the world.

FIVE

# Power, the Expression of God's Love to His Creatures

One of the most common and most harmful errors of our time is that which seeks to oppose the lawful exercise of power to love. This error is the corollary of that which claims to desire to oppose the love of God, men and creation, to detailed obedience to God's commandments.[1] Such errors proceed from the modern notion that love for God and one's neighbor is a *feeling*.[2] No. Contrary to what the prevailing romantic and existentialist humanism claims, true love is not a feeling—which would make it a passive and subjective phenomenon—but *an act of the will directed toward good*. This is what a careful reading of the New Testament compels us to declare. It often speaks of love, but not as a feeling, always an act of the will, regenerated and upheld by God, toward good. The joy of love comes as the fruit of right action. Thus we can clearly affirm that an authority which in its actions conforms to good reveals God's love for His creatures—even, and above all, when it justly punishes those who do evil.

> My son, despise not the chastening of the LORD; neither be weary of his correction: for whom the LORD loveth he correcteth; even as a father the son in whom he delighteth. (Prov. 3:11-12)
>
> If ye endure chastening, God dealeth with you as with

---

[1] Jean-Marc Berthoud, *Apologie pour la Loi de Dieu* (L'Âge d'Homme, Lausanne, 1996). The publication of an English version of this work is forthcoming under the title *In Defense of God's Law* (Zurich Publishing, Tallahassee).

[2] Jean Romain, *La dérive émotionnelle: Essai sur une époque en désarroi* (L'Âge d'Homme, Lausanne, 1998); Digby Anderson and Peter Mullen, eds., *Faking it: The Sentimentalisation of Modern Society* (The Social Affairs Unit, London, 1998).

> sons; for what son is he whom the father chasteneth not?
> . . . [God chastens us] for our profit, that we might be
> partakers of his holiness. (Heb. 12:7, 10)

On the other hand, an authority that refuses to conform to the good, that has no desire to submit to God's Law, unequivocally reveals its rebellion against God and its hatred for God's creatures. It is therefore as the Bible tells us a misguided or bastard authority. "But if ye be without chastisement, whereof all are partakers, then are ye bastards, and not sons" (Heb. 12:8).

Thus, a power that refuses to punish evil is nothing but a power which, instead of working good, works evil.

Moreover, love is by no means the simple feeling that characterizes the position of one who has an attitude of proper submission to the authority of his superiors. Rather, it is his actions, his obedience to lawful demands, that will demonstrate his respect for this authority. This respect and lawful obedience is nothing more than an exact expression of the love a person has for the one who exercises authority over him. Speaking of the behavior (not the feelings) that the Christian woman should bear toward those whom God has rightly placed above her, Paul writes:

> In like manner also, that women adorn themselves . . . (which becometh women professing godliness) with good works. Let the woman learn in silence with all subjection. But I suffer not a woman to teach, nor to usurp authority over the man, but to be in silence. (1 Tim. 2:9-12)

To honor, respect, and lawfully obey is the expression of an individual's love for the person in authority over them. These are not mere feelings but deeds. To consider love first as a feeling and not an act of the will directed toward good can only lead to impeding (or even paralyzing) the Christian's will to act in the world. We won't only render an account to God simply for our feelings and intentions, but above all for our actions, both good and evil. Pietistic sentimentalism effectively leads to the disengagement of Christians from this war that they have an obligation to wage for good against evil. It is through our acts of obedience to God (and not through our feelings) that we are led to fight against sin—within ourselves and outside of ourselves—and this to the point of blood, that is, to the point of martyrdom. To refuse this battle in the name of sentimentalism that cheaply justifies itself is to surrender—without the least struggle—both ourselves and our nations to the domination of Satan. Instead, based on Christ's victory at the cross, we must by faith claim all creation for God, for good, by obeying through the Holy Spirit all the commandments of our Lord Jesus Christ contained in both the Old and New Testaments. This is the only love the gospel recognizes. Thus, through such obedience in love, we will be clothed with the same glorious feelings as those of our Lord Jesus Christ.

SIX

# The Lawful Exercise of the Temporal Power of the Sword is a Preparation for the Kingdom of God

The temporal power's lawful exercise of its God-instituted function to restrain evil by the force of the sword is not in itself the kingdom of God. Yet it can be considered as a preparation or forerunner to the kingdom of God. Power, exercising the lawful restraining function of God's Law, publicly condemns sinful man and visibly upholds—through just judgments handed down in the courts—the distinction God has established between good and evil. In a way, we can say that, in relation to the proclamation of the gospel, temporal power, by its affirmation of the exigencies of the Law of God, exercises a preparatory role toward salvation similar to what John the Baptist did with regard to the Messiah. The sword punishing evil, according to the order established by God's Law, in this way calls people to repentance. It prepares the way of the Lord—who alone brings pardon and forgiveness, granting access into the kingdom of God. This is the tutor that Paul mentions whose task is to lead us to Christ. For it is through faith in Christ alone that we obtain access to the kingdom of God.

> But before faith came, we were kept under the law, shut up unto the faith which should afterwards be revealed. Wherefore the law was our schoolmaster to bring us unto Christ, that we might be justified by faith. (Gal. 3:23-24)[1]

---

[1] This was the role of the Law for Israel, but it seems to us legitimate to more generally extend this narrow role assigned to it by Paul. It is therefore the action of natural law (written within the order of creation) which inspires the conscience of all people and the order of every society to conform to the immutable standards of eternal law, a justice revealed for our instruction in the biblical Torah.

It is partly by the sword of a lawful temporal power that all men are in fact bound under the guard of natural, creational law, waiting for the present manifestation of the kingdom of God. The kingdom of God is in the world, for it is in the world that the Sower spreads the Word from which the kingdom springs. For the latter is made up of regenerate and baptized Gentiles and Jews. Yet the regenerated, the baptized, are at the same time separated from the world, whose prince is Satan, and they are now under the authority of Christ.[2] Their eyes have been opened, they have turned "from darkness to light, and from the power of Satan unto God," and they "receive forgiveness of sins, and inheritance among them which are sanctified by faith" in Christ (Acts 26:18). It is this inheritance, of which the firstfruits are currently manifested in the world, that constitutes the kingdom. The gospel calls Jews to forsake Judaism, pagans to forsake paganism, to become disciples of God and members of the flock of Jesus Christ, the church. Jesus is the Lord of this people and the Shepherd of this flock. The church on earth constitutes the beginning—the heavenly bridgehead—of the coming kingdom of God. The church participates in the suffering and shame Christ partook of in His incarnation. The fulness and glory of the Kingdom will come later.

> Except a man be born again, he cannot see the kingdom of God.... Except a man be born of water and of the Spirit, he cannot enter into the kingdom of God. (John 3:3-5)
>
> Suffer the little children to come unto me, and forbid them not: for of such is the kingdom of God.... Whosoever shall not receive the kingdom of God as a little child, he shall not enter therein. (Mark 10:14-15)

---

[2] Though Satan is the "prince of this world," all power on earth and in heaven has now been given to Christ. We must not forget a) that the *earth* is not the same thing as the *world,* the first being God's creation, the second Satan's system; and b) the church must claim for Christ this absolute sovereignty that He obtained on the cross, to bring souls from the power of Satan to Christ (Acts 26:18). There is something outrageous, even blasphemous, to the title Lindsay and Carlson gave their book: *Satan is Alive and Well on Planet Earth.* All power has been given to Christ in heaven and on earth, and though Satan, "the prince of this world," still unfortunately exercises his power on this earth, his power is *illegitimate* and *usurped*—and, above all, defeated by Christ on the cross. Our faith in Christ must reveal itself in our present victory over the prince of this world (1 John 5:5).

> Blessed be ye poor: for yours is the kingdom of God. (Luke 6:20)
>
> The kingdom of God cometh not with observation: neither shall they say, Lo here! or, lo there! for, behold, the kingdom of God is within you.³ (Luke 17:20-21)
>
> For the kingdom of God is not meat and drink; but righteousness, and peace, and joy in the Holy Ghost. (Rom. 14:17)
>
> For the kingdom of God is not in word, but in power. (1 Cor. 4:20)
>
> For this ye know, that no whoremonger, nor unclean person, nor covetous man, who is an idolater, hath any inheritance in the kingdom of Christ and of God. (Eph. 5:5)
>
> Hath not God chosen the poor of this world rich in faith, and heirs of the kingdom which he hath promised to them that love him? (Jas. 2:5)
>
> For so an entrance shall be ministered unto you abundantly into the everlasting kingdom of our Lord and Saviour Jesus Christ. (2 Pet. 1:11)

Let's look at a practical example of how the effective abrogation of the law by the courts removes from the eyes of a people the condemnation and punishment of evil and, in the long run, fundamentally blunts their sense of the absolute difference between good and evil, thus making the preaching of repentance extremely difficult and repentance itself almost impossible. The example we'll choose, among many others, is that of abortion and abortifacients.

When abortion and abortifacients are legalized—or (which is effectively the same thing) when we stop punishing as murderers those who have abortions and those who perform them—these terrible crimes quickly come to be considered (both by those who

---

³ "Within you," that is, *within Himself, the King*. Before Pentecost, the kingdom could not be *within* the disciples because the Holy Spirit was only *with them* and *on them* and not yet *in them*, for the Holy Spirit had not yet been given. Since Pentecost, the kingdom of God has been within believers and within the world through their faith and obedience.

commit them and those who request them) as nothing more than ordinary surgical procedures. Among other things, this is a crime against the conscience of the woman who has committed such an act because she will have difficulty recognizing what she has done. By legalizing abortion, by making it commonplace through the magistrate's refusal to punish it with the sword as murder, repentance is almost impossible. Since evil can no longer be brought to light, it will permanently poison the souls of many women who, by the impossibility of recognizing the meaning of the atrocious act they have committed, will be driven to anguish, despair, and spiritual (and often even physical) suicide. Such anguish is almost deadlocked, for the means of recognizing sin, God's unchanging Law that teaches us the difference between good and evil, has been removed.

As for men who allow (or coerce) women whom they have impregnated to abort their mutual child, they sink into a horrible moral-deadening and desensitizing hardness, becoming worse than brute beasts. The cauterization of their conscience makes it almost impossible for them to repent. By refusing to assume responsibility for their act of procreation, they come to lose all the honor of their status as a man. The inevitable result is the moral hardening of all and (which goes hand in hand with this) the feminization and homosexualization of society.

When public authority no longer publicly distinguishes the radical difference between good and evil by its civil judgments, it renounces its role as precursor to the kingdom of God. When opinion, supported by faulty law (and this supported by the false teaching of a false church), tells you that what you have done—in this case an act of murder—is a good deed, how can you recognize evil, repent before God, find His forgiveness in Jesus Christ, and do what is right? Ultimately, it is the Christian preaching of the kingdom of God and the Christian life itself that becomes almost impossible. This is the darkness Christ speaks of in which it is no longer possible to work (John 9:4).

The kingdom of God is where God's will is done.

*Thy kingdom come,*
*Thy will be done,*
*In earth*
*As it is in heaven.*

Wherever the will of the Father who is "in heaven" is done, the kingdom of Heaven (or of God) has effectively come to earth. Many Christian circles make the terrible mistake of postponing the coming of this kingdom until *after* the return of Christ. But to do God's will perfectly on this earth is impossible for fallen—and even regenerate—mankind. Christian righteousness is not *our* righteousness (a righteousness that is our own, that we can attain through our own righteous works done outside of Christ or even in Christ); no, our righteousness is the perfect righteousness of *Christ Himself* which is imputed to us and in which we participate through faith in Him, in His work at the cross, as His Word testifies. It is by justification through faith alone in the complete and definitive work of Jesus Christ, by grace alone, that we have access to the kingdom of Righteousness that Christ has acquired for us, to this kingdom of Righteousness which is the kingdom of God. And this faith, if it is true faith, has the effect of allowing us to practice (albeit imperfectly) the works of righteousness of this kingdom. It is at His return that Jesus Christ will enter into the fullness of this kingdom; every knee will then bow before Him. Let us add that without a clear understanding of God's Law-Word, there can be no understanding of the kingdom of God because the order of this kingdom on earth is that of the Law of God.

# SEVEN

# The Limits of Christian Obedience to the Authority Ordained by God

**Divine Power: Rendering Good for Evil**

"Render to Caesar the things that are Caesar's . . ." that is, "Render therefore to all their dues: tribute to whom tribute is due; custom to whom custom; fear to whom fear; honour to whom honour," and render "to God the things that are God's" (Mark 12:17; Rom. 13:7).

That is,

> Hear, O Israel: The L<small>ORD</small> our God is one L<small>ORD</small>: and thou shalt love the L<small>ORD</small> thy God with all thine heart, and with all thy soul, and with all thy might. And these words, which I command thee this day, shall be in thine heart. (Deut. 6:4-6)

> Go ye therefore, and teach all nations, baptizing them in the name of the Father, and of the Son, and of the Holy Ghost: teaching them to observe all things whatsoever I have commanded you. (Matt. 28:19-10)

Tertullian, in his *On Idolatry,* commented on these verses:

> [Render] the image of Caesar, which is on the coin, to Caesar, and the image of God, which is on man, to God; so as to render to Caesar indeed money, to God yourself.
>
> . . . it behooves us to be in all obedience, according to the apostle's precept, "subject to magistrates, and princes, and powers;" but within the limits of discipline,

so long as we keep ourselves separate from idolatry.[1]

In the Sermon on the Mount, Christ teaches us not to resist evil (Matt. 5:39). Although these words do possess a greater scope, Christ addressed them to His disciples in the context of the Roman occupation of Palestine. Far from recommending to Jews oppressed by their Roman overlords a violent rebellion or a physical resistance to the unjust power of the Romans (the "evil" referred to in this verse), Jesus told His disciples to submit to the unjust abuses of the occupying troops. Blows, unlawful demands and labors, forced borrowing, must all be patiently endured. More than that, these "evil men" (who are also created in the image of God and for whom Christ was about to die) must be loved; we must pray for them. God in His patience "maketh his sun to rise on the evil and on the good, and sendeth rain on the just and on the unjust" (Matt. 5:45). Not that the Lord is delaying the fulfillment of His promise, but He "is longsuffering to us-ward, not willing that any should perish, but that all should come to repentance" (2 Pet. 3:9).

These abuses that Jesus counseled His disciples to submit to were in no way lawful services due to the occupying armies by the Jewish people. John the Baptist had defined the righteous behavior of the soldiers in these terms: "Do violence to no man, neither accuse any falsely; and be content with your wages" (Luke 3:14).

Thus Jesus recommended that the Jews submit to the power of the occupying force by bearing with injustice and not by committing injustice or revolting against them, yet neither by obeying any order the Roman power issued against the Law of God. This was the exact opposite of the message of the revolutionary zealots of His day. In fact, contrary to the carnal aspirations of political freedom within the Jewish people, Jesus seemed to call His fellow-countrymen to nothing less than collaboration with the Roman occupying force. This was something to be hated for. But what was His purpose? To render good for evil; do good to those who exploit you. Yet wouldn't all this *simply strengthen the power of the wicked?* Yes, if this is nothing more than public silence, a refusal to demand the public application of God's Law. It is then nothing more than weakness and cowardice. But a thousand times no if we render evil for good by

---

[1] Tertullian, "On Idolatry," in *The Ante-Nicene Fathers,* Volume III, *Latin Christianity: Its Founder Tertullian* (Eerdmans, Grand Rapids, 1976), 70.

the power of the Holy Spirit, thus proclaiming the sovereign power of Jesus Christ to which all power in heaven and on earth has been given. For, by not resisting the evil that is done to us, we offer a powerful witness to the Truth, to the living and powerful Word of God, in order by it to overcome evil with good, lies with Truth, the power of Satan with the sovereign strength of our Lord Jesus Christ.

Paul doesn't tell us anything different than our Lord and King:

> Therefore if thine enemy hunger, feed him; if he thirst, give him drink: for in so doing thou shalt heap coals of fire on his head. Be not overcome of evil, but overcome evil with good. (Rom. 12:20-21; Prov. 25:21-22)

By avenging ourselves, by rendering evil for evil, we are strengthening the self-justification of the one who is unjust to us. By patiently bearing with injustice, and by even rendering good for evil, we labor to defuse the self-justification of the wicked and awaken his hardened conscience. We are working toward God's conversion of the wicked. It is through repentance and regeneration, not mob action and revolution, that God changes injustice into justice. This is how the sinful inhabitants of the Roman Empire, as well as their unjust institutions, were won over to Jesus Christ. On the other hand, the rebellious attitude of the nationalist and revolutionary Jews ended in their appalling and utter failure and annihilation in the destruction of Jerusalem in the year 70 AD.

There is only one type of just violence, and it is that of the powers established by God for punishing the evildoer. It is this violence of God's justice that Jesus suffered at the cross in our place. The Christian must never seek to avenge himself. This certainly doesn't mean that God in His own time will fail to avenge all the acts of injustice suffered by His children. Don't the souls of the martyrs under the alter cry out to God? They ask, "How long, O Lord, holy and true, dost thou not judge and avenge our blood on them that dwell on the earth?" (Rev. 6:10).

Divine vengeance works in three ways:

1. The magistrate is the servant of God to execute vengeance (Rom. 13:4). The sword of the magistrate

punishing the wrongdoer represents God's actual judgment.
2. Where, by weakness or perversion, the powers that be do not punish the evildoer, God sometimes intervenes directly into history to do it. "And immediately the angel of the Lord smote him, because he gave not God the glory: and he was eaten of worms, and gave up the ghost" (Acts 12:23). Thus, God literally strikes men with physical and spiritual wounds.
3. Finally, each person will be judged for their own works. The hope of God's righteous judgment on the wicked who refuse to believe that the divine wrath intended for them struck Jesus Christ is an important element of the Christian hope. This is, of course, the Last Judgment, in which all the evil actions of all people will find their final reward.

To battle against the unjust violence of evil in this world through the physical violence of revolution only leads to *an increase of evil*. All rebellions and revolutions only work to consolidate the structures of injustice that people seek to overthrow with an optimistic and wicked zeal. But the power of Christ, acting through the faith and obedience of Christians offering their bodies in living, holy, and pleasing sacrifices to God, rendering good for evil, obeying the Truth and resisting evil, if need be, to the point of blood, overturned the strongholds of injustice upon which the Roman Empire was founded: idolatry, totalitarian tyranny, abusive state interference in the economy, slavery, corruption, militarism, public immorality, cruelty, abortion, infanticide, etc. All these evils bowed before the faith of the early Christians, before their refusal of the carnal temptation to *physically resist* evil through evil but instead to *spiritually resist* evil by the very power of God, by faith and obedience to God's Law-Word. In this way God manifested Christ's victory over the world and its injustices through the faithfulness of His church.

Indeed, the gates of hell did not prevail against the early church (Matt. 16:18). Nor are they prevailing against the church in Russia suffering for Christ and His righteousness.[2] This is why Paul

---
[2] This paragraph was originally written in 1976. See the testimony edited by Sergiu

could write to the church in Rome: "the God of peace shall bruise Satan under your feet shortly" (Rom. 16:20).

For, even if the whole world were subject to the Evil One (1 John 5:19), He who is in us is greater than he who is in the world (1 John 4:4).

> For this is the love of God, that we keep his commandments: and his commandments are not grievous. For whatsoever is born of God overcometh the world: and this is the victory that overcometh the world, even our faith. Who is he that overcometh the world, but he that believeth that Jesus is the Son of God? (1 John 5:3-5)

Thus, by submitting to God and by resisting the devil, he will flee from us, from our hearts, our families, our schools, our Christian communities, our societies, our misguided jurisprudence, our nations and, finally (when God wills), from the world itself.

---

Grossu, *Vania Moisseieff, le jeune martyr de Volontirovka* (Catacombes, Courbevoie, 1976).

EIGHT

# Silence: Complicity with Evil

Let me make this point very clear. To render good for evil does not mean to stand silently by while wrong is being committed in the name and under the authority of the civil power. Such silence is a repudiation of the Christian's role to proclaim the Truth of the life-giving Word to a dying culture.

Again, an individual can personally put up with the unjust acts of an evil power. But how can the Christian, by his silence and inaction, support the injustices that others endure? Too often the silence and "patience" of Christians, accepting without flinching the injustices suffered by other people, is nothing but cowardly or unconscious complicity with those who commit evil. We must be able to speak—as a Christian—as Aleksandr Solzhenitsyn or Father D. Doudko did in Moscow against the injustices of an unholy power. We must speak as the Danish martyr pastor Kaj Munk did under the German occupation of his country:

> When injustice cries out in the streets, can my Church remain in its corner? The pulpit is a place upon which great responsibility rests. When we ascend into it, we tremble in our clerical robe because there, in the house of God, the Word is free, free not in the sense that we can say what we want, but free because it is the Word that has authority over us. Here reigns a censorship of the mind, and it is a censorship that forces people to speak, not to be silent. Our only fear is failing to be an obedient servant. Jesus is not only the Savior of the individual but also of the entire nation. Of course, the Church is not the place to discuss the world economy, the new Europe, the ideology of the State; but it is the place from which injustice must be banished, where lies must be exposed, where the

poisoning of minds must be pointed out, where mercy is venerated as a source of life, as the pulsation of the hearts of peoples. . . .

When someone wants to turn black into white, tyranny into liberty, lies into truth, violence into justice, as the Germans desire, the Church in no way oversteps her bounds by involving herself "too much" in politics but instead fulfills her duty because it is written, "Thou shalt have no other gods before me!" Honored colleagues and dear sirs, our duty today is to be reckless.[1]

Munk's courageous words, faithful to the gospel, earned him the glory of martyrdom on January 4, 1944.

On the other hand, pastors and Christians of our own day for the most part live "such an accommodating, such a modernity-driven life, with so little in it to displease modern pagans, that they are very unlikely to ever be persecuted."[2] We deify the state, which has become the Sovereign in our eyes, the source of all law and property. The words that the twelfth-century Byzantine courtier addressed to the emperor could easily be adapted to our present idolatry of the welfare state:

> On earth, there is no distinction between the power of God and the power of the Emperor. Rulers possess the right to do anything; and without reservation they can employ what belongs to God as if it belonged to themselves. For they received the imperial investiture from God, and between God and them there is no longer any distinction.[3]

When, then will Christians realize that we are not far from such an effective deification of the humanist state devoid of God, whose religion is the worship of the individual and collective man (whose theoretical expression is found in the ideology of "human

---

[1] Gudrun Cavin, *Kaj Munk: dramaturge, prophète et martyr* (Geneva: Labor et Fides, 1945). See also Kaj Munk, *La Croix sur l' étendard: Paroles sous l'oppression* (Paris, 1945). We also highly recommend J. Maarten's book, *Le village sur la montagne: Tableau de l'Église fidèle sous le règne nazi* (Geneva, 1940).
[2] R. Barilier, pastor, *Nouvelle Revue de Lausanne,* June 25, 1977.
[3] R. L. Bruckberger, *Dieu et la politique* (Plon, Paris, 1971), 65.

rights")⁴ and whose official "church" is none other than secular compulsory education, a de facto anti-Christian school because it utterly rejects the testimony of the Word of God?

---

⁴ Jean-Marc Berthoud, *Une religion sans Dieu.*

# NINE

# Obedience to God

But let us hasten to add that under no circumstances does Jesus permit His disciples to commit injustice or unrighteousness themselves by commanding them to have such an attitude of submission and patience toward the injustices they suffer. That is, submission to the powers established by God can never be a pretext for doing the evil that these powers might order us to do or for neglecting to do the good that these powers might forbid us from doing, for "we ought to obey God rather than men" (Acts 5:29).

We must be subject to the powers that God has established because this is His will and this is the order He has established among mankind. But we must obey the supreme power, God, by always faithfully accomplishing everything that He has commanded us to do.

Power, such as is described for us in Romans 13:1-7, is the power that enforces God's Law, that punishes the wrongdoer and approves the one who does good. In Scripture, good and evil are always defined by God—that is, by divine Law. Thus, unlike all the legal teaching currently given in the institutions of higher learning (the teaching that the law is merely an autonomous creation of a sovereign human legislator), laws must always be subject to the binding normative requirements of God's Law.[1]

Thus, if the power established by God commands us to do things which are not contrary to God's Law, even if we are forced to endure abuse, as long as these unjust constraints *do not compel us to acts of injustice,* we must (if we have no lawful recourse) not only respectfully submit to power, but *we must obey it.* Yet our submission to the injustice we suffer in no way implies that we remain silent in

---

[1] We must remember that the so-called "natural law" (the foundation of personal conscience and jurisprudence) has always had its basis in the eternal law of God, of which biblical Law is the divinely-revealed, normatively-infallible expression which is well adapted by the Holy Spirit to the limited abilities of men.

the face of similar injustices suffered by others.

A typical example is that of the Russian Orthodox Christian Igor Shafarevich, who unjustly lost his chair in mathematics at Moscow University for ideological and religious reasons. He thought it appropriate to remain silent in the face of the blatant injustice he suffered. Shortly thereafter, at a seminar he attended (organized by one of his students), his student also suffered the same affront, being dismissed for equally spurious reasons. Igor Shafarevitch did not hesitate to react and to use his international scientific reputation to denounce this injustice before the entire world. This example is a model of what the action of a faithful Christian should be.

On the other hand, if a misguided power orders us to commit unjust acts (contrary to God's Law), *we must disobey man in order to obey God*. If we can't flee elsewhere or hide, we will have to submit with faith to the unjust measures that the authorities will take against us. It is by the strength of the Holy Spirit that we disobey the wicked injunctions of a misguided and evil power. And in this way we will victoriously resist the Evil One—if necessary at the cost of martyrdom—by persevering in obedience to the Word of God.

**Biblical Examples**

Examples of this disobedience to men in order to offer first obedience to God can be found throughout the Bible. In the face of unjust civil powers, we see men of the Bible, fearing God more than men, manifesting their faith by disobeying the unjust abuses of an iniquitous power. See how Moses behaved before Pharaoh, Jonathan before his father (and king) Saul, Elijah facing Ahab and Jezebel, and Daniel before the unrighteous demands of Darius. In each of these cases we see a shining example of the behavior God demands of us: obedience to God and disobedience to unjust power, though this must be performed in a spirit of submission and respect to the earthly power.

In the New Testament we find this same attitude among the Magi and John the Baptist before Herod. In Jesus Christ Himself, we see to the highest degree the presence of this double attitude. We never see Him obey the ungodly and unjust demands of the leaders of the Jewish people who demanded that He cease from obeying His Father; that He no longer proclaim the good news of the kingdom of God; and that He perform no more wondrous works of His

Heavenly Father. In particular, we see Him in an almost provocative way refusing to obey the prohibitions of the scribes and Pharisees—whose tradition had overthrown divine Law—from doing good on the Sabbath. Christ's fulfillment of the works of divine mercy on the Sabbath demonstrated its true meaning, for the Sabbath was the figure *par excellence* of the kingdom of God. We also see the vehement manner in which Jesus opposed the distortions to which the Jewish leaders subjected the Law of God, following their tradition of men, as well as His public denunciation of their hypocrisy. He called them "whitewashed sepulchers" and didn't hesitate on two occasions to drive the moneychangers and merchants out of the temple. Thus He exercised discipline in the house of God (His own house!) in the place of the priests who should have done this.

And, though He didn't hesitate to state the facts just as clearly to the public authorities—even calling Herod a "fox"—yet when He was asked to execute justice, for example to hand down a ruling on the division of an inheritance, Jesus replied: "Who made me a judge or a divider over you?" (Luke 12:14). In saying this, He confirmed in the clearest way possible the biblical distinction between the two powers: spiritual power (His at the time of the incarnation), and temporal power (which the man wrongly desired Him to assume). But, despite these numerous acts of public resistance to injustice manifesting itself in various ways, we never see Jesus pressing His disciples either to a direct challenge of political authority or to a spirit of rebellion, let alone inciting them to a political battle, social demands, or revolutionary acts.[2] We find strong opposition to injustice in Jesus, but never revolt against authority. He knew well that if man's heart was not first changed, the kingdom of God could not be revealed. On the contrary, He even confirmed the authority of the scribes and Pharisees (though not their injustices!) when He declared to the people and His disciples: "The scribes and the Pharisees sit in Moses' seat: all therefore whatsoever they bid you observe, that observe and do; but do not ye after their works: for they say, and do not" (Matt. 23:2-3).

And, despite the blatant hypocrisy of the leaders of Israel—

---

[2] Whoever refuses to obey ungodly laws in order to obey God, whether in the church or in the world, is never a rebel. A rebel is one who revolts against the Law of God, against God Himself. Too often today, those who hold power are themselves the real rebels. In no way should we confuse just resistance, a spiritual and practical opposition to injustice, with a challenge to power and a revolution against institutions.

which, in our carnal eyes, would free us from any respect we owed to their authority—He refused to encourage the people to any incitement to revolution.

For, for Jesus (and all the more for us), the political struggle is not a dualistic battle against power as an institution of creation—which would make it a Gnostic battle against God who Himself established this institution—but a spiritual and temporal battle against the evil powers which, through the injustices of men, have in fact taken possession of the political sphere. And, when the guards of the Sanhedrin seized Him to put Him to death, He neither defended Himself nor incited a rebellion. He knew that the weakness of God is stronger than the power of men. He disarmed His disciples and explicitly refused to call the heavenly army to His assistance, which was ready at His command.[3] Having said all that His Father had commanded Him to say, having accomplished all that His Father had commanded Him to do, He was "brought as a lamb to the slaughter, and as a sheep before her shearers is dumb, so he openeth not his mouth" (Isa. 53:7).

It is this weakness of Jesus Christ crucified that has conquered all the powers of evil, that has conquered the world and the force of injustice in the world. It is this victory of the weakness of God over the powers of this world that allows even the restoration of this power in the just exercise of its creational functions.

We see Christ's disciples doing the same. The Sanhedrin excommunicated from Israel all those who followed Jesus. The disciples chose to obey Jesus and disobey the leaders of their people. The Pharisees sought to put Jesus to death and bribe His disciples to betray Him. The leaders of the Jewish people found no one but Judas Iscariot who was willing to obey them rather than God. But, with the exception of the case of Peter during Jesus' arrest (when he drew his sword to defend his Master), we never see the disciples adopt the revolutionary attitude of a Barabbas or that of the nationalist and revolutionary zealots in the face of the "collaborative" power of their

---

[3] This behavior of non-resistance to evil on the part of the Lord Jesus Christ is the very opposite of the pseudo-Christian "pacifism" of Louis XVI who forbade his Swiss guard in Versailles from using their arms against the mob and thereby in fact ordered their massacre; or Nicolas II, the Russian tsar, commander-in-chief of the Russian armies, who ordered his Cossack troops not to fire on the enraged crowds on the streets of Saint Petersburg during the 1905 revolution. Both are clear cases of dereliction of duty on the part of the supreme military chief of these nations.

time or against the Roman occupying forces.

After Pentecost, the apostles persevered in this obedience to God and in this disobedience, that of disobeying and resisting the wicked orders of Jewish authority, though always in an attitude of submission and respect. Since God had given the disciples the order to proclaim the good news of the kingdom, it was not in the power of the authorities established by this same God to prevent them from doing so. Thus, even though the high priest expressly reminded them of the peremptory orders of the Sanhedrin: "Did we not straitly command you that ye should not teach in this name?" (Acts 5:28), yet the disciples had received from the Lord another even more compelling order: "Go therefore and make disciples of all the nations, baptizing them in the name of the Father and of the Son and of the Holy Spirit, teaching them to observe all things that I have commanded you" (Matt. 28:19-20).

A confirmation of this order had been given to the apostles by the angel who freed them from prison and who ordered: "Go, stand and speak in the temple to the people all the words of this life" (Acts 5:20).

The result was that, according to the statement of the high priest himself, they had "filled all Jerusalem" with their teaching (Acts 5:28). What else could they say before the iniquitous power of the Sanhedrin than what Peter and the other apostles answered: "We ought to obey God rather than men" (Acts 5:29)?

But here again, never do we see this disobedience to men, this opposition to injustice, this resistance to sin, perhaps even to the point of blood, accompanied by challenges to power or acts of revolution or violence. Rather, these words of Peter were their watchword:

> And who is he that will harm you, if ye be followers of that which is good? But and if ye suffer for righteousness' sake, happy are ye: and be not afraid of their terror, neither be troubled; but sanctify the Lord God in your hearts: and be ready always to give an answer to every man that asketh you a reason of the hope that is in you with meekness and fear: having a good conscience; that, whereas they speak evil of you, as of evildoers, they may be ashamed that falsely accuse your good conversation in Christ. For it is better, if the will of God be so, that ye

suffer for well doing, than for evil doing. (1 Pet. 3:13-17)

Jesus, addressing Peter who with his sword had just cut off the ear of the servant of the high priest—a picture of all violent rebellion against the power established by God—said, "all they that take the sword shall perish with the sword," thus condemning once and for all any so-called Christianity—either reactionary or revolutionary—that seeks to restore a "reign of justice" through the use of revolution (or counter-revolution) and violence (Matt. 26:52).

When Christ affirms that it is the violent who will take the kingdom of God and that we enter it through violence, He is obviously speaking of a violence that we must exert *against ourselves*, against the sin within us, and in no way a violence exercised to force others to enter by constraint into the kingdom of God (Matt. 11:12). For, though this kingdom is earthly (on earth), yet it is spiritual and not carnal.

Even in the face of the utterly anti-Christian power symbolized by the beasts of Revelation 13, all violent revolution is forbidden. "He that killeth with the sword must be killed by the sword" expresses the condemnation of those who take up the sword against the people of God, for God will with the sword justly avenge His disciples (Rev. 13:10). For, in the face of evil, our action must not be to overthrow this evil by our carnal forces, but we must *suffer patiently* for good if this is God's will, and *by faith* move the mountains of iniquity that stand in our way.

As Pastor R. J. Rushdoony put it very well, God did not call men to a gospel of revolution but of regeneration which, by the peaceful obedience of the regenerated to God, to His Law-Word, the beginnings of the kingdom of God are established on earth.[4] Faced with ungodly and unjust powers, the Christian *does not revolt*, yet *nor does he obey* this power of injustice. Under the blows of the enemy, he resists spiritually, *he bends with patience, exercising his faith* that, on the day desired by God, God will lift him up and give him victory. "Humble yourselves therefore under the mighty hand of God, that he may exalt you in due time: casting all your care upon him; for he careth for you" (1 Pet. 5:6-7).

---

[4] R. J. Rushdoony, *The Institutes of Biblical Law,* Volume One (Presbyterian and Reformed, Philadelphia, 1973), 413.

TEN

# Contemporary Practical Examples

Let's look at some examples of this obligatory obedience (in a spirit of submission) of those who seek to see in their Christian lives the fruits of justice—that is, obedience to God.[1]

**Business**

A Christian employee or businessman cannot obey orders from his superiors that require him to engage in malfeasance or fraud. In a respectful spirit, he must first peacefully seek to dissuade his superiors from taking such actions. This must be done in a spirit of faith and supplication to God. If this attempt fails, he must simply refuse to obey such orders while peacefully accepting the consequences of such an act.

There are three things to consider here.

First, faith in obedience to God's demands can and must win victories that will result in the amelioration of our economic world.

Secondly, a fight of this magnitude against the evil powers that hold the business world captive to injustice is not solely the work of the person engaged in it. *The prayer and faith of the local church must also be behind such a struggle,* for it is against the church of God—not against the isolated Christian in his struggles—that the gates of hell will not prevail.

Thirdly, it is essential that the church provide teaching on business life that is both fundamentally biblical and fully conscious of economic realities, so that the Christians who attend such a

---

[1] Two collective works are essential here: Gary North, ed., *The Theology of Christian Resistance* (Geneva Divinity School Press, Tyler, Texas, 1983) and Gary North, ed., *Tactics of Christian Resistance* (Geneva Divinity School Press, Tyler, Texas, 1983). See also Jean-Marc Berthoud, *Les Dix Commandements lus par la Bible: Une Lumière divine pour notre temps: Le huitième commandement: Tu ne voleras pas: L'Économie, Le Vol et l'Ordre de la Création* (Messages, Lausanne, Lulu.com, 2019).

church know how to conduct themselves in this realm of business.[2]

**The Medical Profession**

A Christian nurse or doctor who is ordered by a superior to assist in an abortion must, while maintaining a submissive and respectful attitude, absolutely refuse to obey. If a Christian complies with such an order in a spirit of false submission, he becomes an accomplice to a murder and will be judged by God for it. To illustrate the proper biblical response to such a dilemma, we will quote the highly instructive reaction of hospital healthcare staff in the context of the battle against abortion in Switzerland:

> We the general care nurses, psychiatric nurses, assistant nurses, and midwives, the undersigned, declare that we condemn any legislation permitting abortion or the termination of pregnancy.
>
> We subscribe to the Declaration of the Swiss Association of Physicians for the Respect of Life, in which it is stated in particular, "the first duty of medicine is to respect every human being's right to life, regardless of his illness, infirmity, age, intelligence, or social status. . . . To terminate a pregnancy to resolve a moral, psychological, economic, or social conflict is not the act of a doctor."
>
> A deliberate termination of pregnancy, even permitted by law, always constitutes a homicide contrary to the fundamental nature of professional ethics. It is therefore unacceptable in good conscience to participate in it.[3]

Here again, the Christian must peacefully accept the consequences such a refusal may bring with it. Again, the persuasive force

---

[2] A remarkable example of such teaching can be found in the commentaries on the Decalogue by Pierre Viret (*Exposition of the Ten Commandments*, two volumes, published by Psalm 78 Ministries, 2020) and R. J. Rushdoony (*Institutes of Biblical Law*, three volumes, Ross House Books). See also André Biéler, *La pensée économique et sociale de Calvin* (Georg, Geneva, 1961); Étienne Catta, *La doctrine politique et sociale du Cardinal Pie* (Nouvelles Éditions Latines, Paris, 1991 [1957]); and Jean Daujat, *L'ordre social chrétien* (Beauchesne, Paris, 1970). The works of Wilhelm Röpke and Gary North (almost all published by the Institute for Christian Economics and freely available on the internet) are of great interest for an understanding of the Christian sense of economic realities.

[3] *Déclaration de l'Association suisse du personnel infirmier et des sages-femmes pour le respect de la vie*. This text dates from the mid-1970s.

of the Truth must not be minimized, ever supported by a gentle and peaceful but unwavering determination not to engage in evildoing. Nor should we forget that it is through faith that the situation must change from evil to good. Here again such a battle must be illuminated by the realistic and genuine preaching of the church, by the faith and prayer of the local body of Christ. The task of a Christian nurse, a Christian physician, and the church is by no means to diminish, weaken, or much less attempt to destroy the power of the medical hierarchy, but rather to labor to cleanse and restore this power to its only true foundations: submission and conformity to God's commandments.[4]

**The Police**

A police officer—like any other person for that matter—is under the law, not only under the positive law of existing civil law, but also under the immutable and normative Law of God. His task is to resist evil, to bring evildoers to justice, and to encourage those who do good by maintaining public peace and order. This is why the church is called to pray for the powers that be, in order that peace might be maintained and the kingdom of God might be proclaimed. But a Christian police officer may find himself in a situation in which his superiors demand him to act—whether legally or illegally is inconsequential—contrary to God's Law. For example, his superiors may require him to torture or abuse prisoners in his custody. Or perhaps, more common in my home country of Switzerland, they may require him to ignore the offenses of persons in positions of authority. If he obeys his superiors, he puts himself in the place of the magistrate, who alone has the power of punishment or exoneration. But, even more, by obeying his superiors he violates the Law of God (which is a much more grievous offense) and becomes liable to the court of God's justice.

Again, a Christian police officer finds himself in a difficult situation in which he must obey God rather than men while ever remaining submissive in his attitude to the authority of his superiors. With what fervency should the church of God pray for our police

---

[4] See Franklin E. Payne, *Biblical Medical Ethics: The Christian and the Practice of Medicine* (Mott Media, Milford, Michigan, 1985); Nigel M. de S. Cameron, *The New Medicine: Life and Death After Hippocrates* (Crossway Books, Wheaton, Illinois, 1992); John M. Frame, *Medical Ethics: Principles, Persons and Problems* (Presbyterian and Reformed, Philadelphia, 1988).

force, that it might faithfully fulfill its task according to the dictates of Jesus Christ, and that it might not become—by passivity in the face of public evil or by active evil in the discharge of its duties—an agent of the power of iniquity![5]

### The Magistrate

A Christian magistrate finds himself in a particularly difficult—we might even say impossible—situation in our own day when all regimes, both "democratic" or "totalitarian," have without exception substituted the sovereignty of the "people," the "party," or the "leader" for the sovereignty of God and His Law *transcendent over all*. The magistrate, such as he is described in Romans 13, can most certainly be a Christian, enforcing the law, punishing the evildoer and rewarding those who do good, while always remaining *under the immutable and absolute Law of God*. But what about when times become evil, when "all the foundations of the earth are out of course" (Ps. 82:5) and judges "judge unjustly, and accept the persons of the wicked" (Ps. 82:2)? And what about when those who should render justice and who should "defend the poor and fatherless: do justice to the afflicted and needy" instead "know not, neither will they understand," but "walk on in darkness" (Ps. 82:2-5)?

What about when the civil power which should only apply justice as defined by God's Law (appropriately applied to time and place) replaces God with itself as the source of law and becomes a law to itself, thus changing evil into good and good into evil? Our parliaments and legislatures have long declared themselves to be a source of law. They can declare anything—just or unjust—to be law, and the magistrate is then obligated to enforce that law. The magistrate's task is unenviable, for it is he who must put such laws into execution, ultimately *encouraging the evildoer* and *punishing those who do good*. A Christian magistrate who does not wish to be judged by God for his evil works as an iniquitous judge on the Last Day has no choice but to refuse to enforce such iniquitous laws. It seems to me that, as Nicolas de Flue (1417-1487) did, he will have to withdraw from the court of justice to pray and labor, so that God might restore a situation in which justice can once again become a public reality.[6]

---

[5] See John W. Whitehead, *Battlefield America: The War on the American People,* foreword by Ron Paul (SelectBooks, 2015).
[6] On these issues, see the above-mentioned works of Pierre Viret and Rousas J. Rush-

**The Christian and the Armed Forces**[7]

If God has given the civil magistrate the power of the sword to uphold the peace and order willed by God within the territory under his jurisdiction, we must also clearly affirm that military power also proceeds from God. Its purpose is to protect the country in which its power is exercised from foreign countries that seek to harm it. Again, any challenge to military power as such is a challenge to God Himself, Master of the heavenly armies. But, like all power, military power must be subject to God's order, to God's Law. The Christian therefore can no more deny the divine ordinance of military power as a power established by God for the protection of the inhabitants of his country against *foreign evildoers* than he can deny the power of the magistrate who by God's authority bears the sword to punish the *evildoers within his country*. These powers are established by God because of the sin of mankind. Therefore those who, by idealistic pacifism, labor for their abolition do so because they no longer see, in their idealistic blindness, the creational nature of political institutions and the radically sinful nature of all men.

To take a recent example, after the suicide of a conscientious objector in prison, we saw young pacifists brandishing the slogan "Prison kills. Kill prison!" This is the purest form of Rousseau's ideology: evil proceeds from the institution and not the heart of man. According to this philosophy, we must merely overturn the institutions that kill, and man will be regenerated. The result: the Terror of the French Revolution, the Bolshevik Gulag Archipelago and, today, the riots on the streets of many cities across the United States.

Those who work for the abolition of police and military power in their country—if they aren't being bribed by foreign powers—are possessed by a utopian vision of the natural goodness of man, a completely unrealistic and gravely dangerous vision. For they

---

doony. See also E. L. Hebden Taylor's little book, *The New Legality in the Light of the Christian Philosophy of Law*. See also the references in our study, "Saint Thomas Aquinas and politics" in *L'Histoire Alliancielle de l'Église dans le Monde*, Volume 2 (Messages, Lausanne, Lulu.com, 2019), as well as Lancelot Andrewes' commentary on the Ten Commandments, *An Exposition Upon the Ten Commandments* (Richard Cotes, London, 1642) and the works of Friedrich Julius Stahl on the philosophy of the law, *Die Philosophy of the Rechts nach geschichtlicher Unsicht* (J. C. B. Mohr, Heidelberg, 1830-1837).

[7] Henry Chavannes, *L'objection de conscience* (Cahiers de la Renaissance Vaudoise, Lausanne, 1961).

labor—consciously or unconsciously—to deliver their country into the hands of the most voracious and most powerful foreign military power, just as those who work toward the dismantling of civil power work to deliver defenseless law-abiding citizens into the hands of criminals. Moved by unrealistic, wicked optimism, all these utopian idealists who deny the reality of sin in all men work to destroy the authority structures established by God for the good of men.

We must repeat: *the power of the sword is a blessing and a good.*

But we can ask ourselves how the Christian—whose duty before God is to render good for evil and thus overcome evil with good—can have any part in this work of earthly justice which is to repress evil by the violence of the power of the sword, a sword that is applied to the evildoer (dwelling within the country) by the police and the aggressor (from outside the country) by the army? We must first make it very clear that the use of the power of the sword—whether by the police or the army—when subject to the standards of God's Law *is by no means an evil but rather a great good established by God for the normal development of human life in society.* Contrary to popular opinion, violence in itself is not evil.[8] Legitimate violence that represses evil (and which is nothing more than God's righteousness manifested here on earth) is a divine blessing. Violence itself is not the definition of evil; evil is any violation of God's Law. This is why we never see the Bible condemning the legitimate exercise of the just power of the sword, a power whose aim is to suppress the criminal actions of evildoers both within and outside the country. We never see Jesus or His apostles recommending to soldiers who have become converted to the gospel to leave their profession (which is violent by nature) as a precondition to their entrance into the Christian life.

Here we must point out that it in two Roman military officers that we find exemplary testimonies of piety, justice, and faith. Of the pagan centurion of Capernaum, Jesus made this astonishing statement, "Verily I say unto you, I have not found so great faith, no, not in Israel" (Matt. 8:10).

---

[8] Even such a scholar as Jacques Ellul fell into this utopian antinomian pacifism. See his book *Contre les violents* (Centurion, Paris, 1972), in which the just violence of authority is not distinguished from the violence of evildoers. The same is true, though in an exacerbated way, of Pope Benedict XVI.

Yet we never see Jesus in any way recommending to that career officer to abandon his military position as a condition of following Him. The same is true of Cornelius, the Roman centurion of Caesarea, whose conversion paved the way for the preaching of the gospel to the heathen. While faithfully exercising the military profession—a profession whose foundation finds its establishment in God Himself—he was, as Scripture tells us, "a devout man, and one that feared God with all his house, which gave much alms to the people, and prayed to God alway" (Acts 10:2).

Within the course of this narrative which tells of Cornelius' conversion to the gospel and the coming of the Holy Spirit on all those in his house who listened to the Apostle Peter's preaching of the Word, we find that the Holy Spirit acted in exactly the same way as when He first descended on the disciples at Pentecost. Moreover, we never see Peter recommending that Cornelius in any way abandon his military career, a profession whose faithful exercise allowed him to be "a just man, and one that feareth God, and of good report among all the nation of the Jews" (Acts 10:22).

When the soldiers ("men of war" in the original) asked John the Baptist, "And what shall we do?" he never encouraged them to leave the profession of arms to embrace a utopian pacifism, but instead he said to them: "Do violence to no man, neither accuse any falsely; and be content with your wages" (Luke 3:14).

Basically, what he said to the soldiers was that the power of the sword they exercised—a perfectly legitimate power—must, like any other position of authority, be exercised under the control of the Law and not independently or in defiance of God's Law.

As British Rear Admiral Clarence Howard-Johnston said during a conversation with his porter on the platform of the Lausanne train station, within the English navy a military order must be rational, morally legitimate, and not criminal before it can be obeyed.[9] This is the heart of the difference between the absolute (unconditional) discipline of the French army and the discipline—sub-

---

[9] In this same Lausanne station, this porter had the opportunity to speak two days in a row, with travelers, one Polish and the other Romanian, who had exercised high judicial functions in their countries before the arrival of communism. They were both forced to choose between either pursuing their careers or refusing to comply with the iniquitous orders of the Communist Party and thus cover political crimes with their legal authority. The consequence of their refusal to be accomplices in wicked judgments was the destruction of their careers and being relegated to the harsh lives of manual laborers.

ject to the condition that the orders are "lawful"—which prevails in the British army. Here are two historical examples of this difference, both taken from Switzerland:

1. During World War II, Jewish refugees were turned back at the German/Swiss border, from which they were then escorted to the death camps.
2. Cossack refugees from Vlassov's army who had collaborated with German troops during the war claimed political asylum in Switzerland in 1944 after laying down their arms in the border town of Vallorbe. They were immediately loaded onto military trucks and were driven back to another point along the border with France, where they were handed over to Communist guerrillas who executed them.

In these two cases, the iniquitous orders leading to the extermination of defenseless men in order to defend a policy of neutrality—that is, of appeasement with regard to the dominant power of the moment—should have been refused by those who received them, if they did not wish to stand in solidarity with the intrinsically evil acts they were asked to perform. Even such a man as Theodore Roosevelt recognized the truth of this when he quipped: "To be neutral between right and wrong is to serve wrong."[10]

The conclusion is clear. The Christian soldier is never obligated to *unconditionally* submit to the orders he receives from his military superiors. Normally he owes them obedience, an obedience without which the armed forces could not exist. But it may be that in certain circumstances a Christian is driven, not to "conscientious objection"—which is nothing more than the refusal to fulfill his duty to serve in the name of the revolt of an *autonomous conscience* independent of God's Law—but simply to the refusal to obey an iniquitous military order. Animated by a gentle and teachable (and not a violent and revolutionary) spirit, he must disobey the morally perverse order of his military superiors in order to obey God before all. In the early church, when a Christian soldier or officer was obligated to swear an oath to the emperor that included an act of idola-

---

[10] Quoted in Edmond Morris, *Colonel Roosevelt* (Random House, New York, 2010), 396.

try toward him, he could do nothing but refuse this unholy order, a refusal which (at the time) frequently led to martyrdom. In such circumstances, a Christian could only refuse the order, choosing to obey God rather than men, even if the price was death. This was the choice made by the Theban legion exterminated at Saint Maurice in Valais (Switzerland) during the Diocletian persecution at the end of the third century.[11] It is equally clear that a Christian soldier or officer cannot accept or obey orders which are openly contrary to divine Law without grievously sinning against God and against his neighbor.[12]

But it is also not possible for a Christian soldier to seek to evade the normal military consequences of his refusal of obedience by declaring the military to be invalid. For, by trying to legitimize his refusal to obey the draft order by establishing a kind of civil service that would replace his obligation to serve, he only exacerbates his disobedience. Having refused to obey a draft notice, he must appear before the military courts of his country to attempt to legally justify his refusal, where he will have the opportunity to testify freely of his membership in another kingdom—the Heavenly Kingdom—and his engagement in another war (that of a spiritual nature). This kingdom and this war, the stakes of which are nothing less than the eternal salvation of mankind, are much more demanding than that whose purpose is the defense of an earthly homeland. This is why a Christian who appears before a military court for legitimately refusing to obey an order will only be able to peacefully—and without revolt against the power of the armed forces—accept the sanction that will be imposed on him. The legitimate refusal of an immoral, criminal, or ungodly order should in no way induce him to reject the military institution itself. It is injustice that must be refused and not the institution. For the Christian does not seek (as the pacifist conscientious objector) to destroy the military power but rather to cleanse and strengthen it so that it may be able to accomplish the indispensable task for which God ordained it. Moreover, by his action he testifies to his belonging to another kingdom, the kingdom of God, which has now drawn near to men. The non-Christian citizen

---

[11] See Jean-Marc Berthoud, "Le martyre de la légion thebaine: Saint Maurice et le combat contre le paganisme" in *Des Actes de l'Église: Le christianisme en Suisse romande* (L'Âge d'Homme, Lausanne, 1993), 13-21.

[12] Any military oath which would have the effect of freeing the one who takes it from his obedience to the Law of God must be refused by Christians.

only possesses one homeland.[13] The Christian, on the other hand, finds himself placed between two homelands: one earthly, to which he has relative obligations, and the other heavenly, which demands from him an absolute commitment. When a choice is required between the two—normally an exceptional choice—the first and last loyalty of the faithful Christian can only be to his heavenly homeland. Speaking of those who died in the faith—often under the blows of a misguided earthly authority, "not having received the promises," the author of the epistle to the Hebrews tells us:

> These [the martyrs of the Old Covenant and *a fortiori* those of the New] confessed that they were strangers and pilgrims on the earth. For they that say such things declare plainly that they seek a country. And truly, if they had been mindful of that country from whence they came out, they might have had opportunity to have returned. But now they desire a better country, that is, an heavenly: wherefore God is not ashamed to be called their God: for he hath prepared for them a city. (Heb. 11:13-16)

It is from this perspective and with this hope that we are often required—and that in the midst of grave combat—to obey God rather than men.

**The Teaching Profession**

Since the virtual universalization of the state monopoly of education and its consequent secularization (i.e., the exclusion of all transcendent standards) of all subjects taught, it is either forbidden or increasingly difficult for Christian teachers in public schools to

---

[13] Here, we seek to define the principles. It is clear that a Christian cannot stand in solidarity with aggressive nationalist or ideological wars. Although, to a greater or lesser extent, this has always been the case, modern nationalism, as well as the pressure of international finance on the politics of states, have profoundly diverted the armed forces from their well-defined goal: to defend the homeland. This fundamental notion of homeland is now drowned in the internationalism of our new Tower of Babel whose main institutions are the United Nations and UNESCO. The notion of homeland is often similarly diverted from its proper end by idolatrous nationalism that destroys its reality. We must add that the truly diabolical development of modern weapons of mass destruction pose serious moral problems that we will not deal with here but which make us understand (though without fully approving of them) that certain Christians cannot accept a profession within the military service. Modern military techniques amplify the problem but do not change the facts.

speak of God, the God of the Bible, to their students. The textbooks of all branches are designed with an atheistic worldview in which there is no longer any place for God.

> The fool hath said in his heart, There is no God. They are corrupt, they have done abominable works, there is none that doeth good. . . . They are all gone aside, they are all together become filthy: there is none that doeth good, no, not one. Have all the workers of iniquity no knowledge? (Ps. 14:1-4)

Does the Christian teacher have the right—out of fear of the authority that hired him—to stand before his class and behave like this madman, this fool of whom David speaks, by excluding all reference to God from his teaching? If he does, he will be no different than the sinners spoken of by the Apostle Paul who hold the truth in unrighteousness and who stand inexcusable before God, for "when they knew God, they glorified him not as God, neither were thankful; but became vain in their imaginations, and their foolish heart was darkened. Professing themselves to be wise, they became fools" (Rom. 1:21-22).

For the Christian teacher, this is the inevitable result of his blind obedience to the ungodly instructions of his "secular" superiors. The teaching of such Christians will in the long run be marked by lies and deceit, for in all that they tell their students they will have excluded from their thoughts the One in whom the understanding and meaning of all things is found. For it is He, Jesus Christ, the Word of God, who is the Creator of all things, the Light of the world, who through creation has given meaning to all that exists and in whose light we see and understand everything. This is the dilemma faced by Christian teachers in secular schools. And we must unfortunately add that "Christian" schools often scarcely mention the Creator in the teaching they provide to the children of Christian families! A Christian instructor in secular territory must either obey the unholy instructions and manuals of the leaders of a school without God and in rebellion against God, and thus participate personally in this ungodliness, or he must seek with prudence to obey God rather than men. Without fear, without rebellion, but in a spirit of strength and peace, he must—against the spirit of the institution that hired him—proclaim God's sovereignty over all His creatures, the reign of divine Providence over history and the works of men—that is, over every aspect of the subject matter of all his teaching.

This is a situation that forces the Christian teacher in a secular environment to make clear choices. But how will this choice be made if the church doesn't teach such teachers first to discern and then to walk faithfully in this narrow path? How can a teacher lead a life of obedience that requires so much faith, discernment, and courage if the leaders of the church are not leading the sheep (whom God has entrusted to them) to unfailing faith; if they do not labor to make them mature Christians, strengthened for the accomplishment of every good work; and if such a difficult fight is not supported by the prayers of this same church?

But, armed with a valiant and faithful church, God will lead His disciples—even in positions of secular instruction—to win this victory of faith over the world that Christ has purchased for all His children at the cross of Golgotha and, by exercising this faith, to bring every thought captive to the obedience of Christ. It is through winning such victories that the faithful will lay hold of the crown of glory.[14]

**In the Church**

In the church also the power established by God is not infallible. Not even the church can claim *unconditional* obedience from us. Again, when we are faced with constraints contrary to the teaching of God's Word, we have the responsibility to obey God rather than men. We cannot, without surrendering ourselves into the hands of *fallible men,* pretend that we owe unconditional obedience to the ministers of God in His church. The tradition of men, human regulations, and human structures are one thing, and the ordinance of God expressed in His infallible Word is another. We must judge our traditions, regulations, and our structuring of churches and works in the light of Scripture alone. Examining all things in this way, we must reject error and evil and retain and obey the true and the good alone. Yet we must not allow our individual examination of biblical Truth to become a pretext for refusing the authority of the ministers of the church and thus attempting to live according to the dictates of the flesh. This would be nothing more than an ideological veil created to cover the unsubmissive will still present in the believer,

---

[14] See Jean-Marc Berthoud, *L'école et la famille contre l'utopie.*

rejecting the authorities established by God for His church. Anti-ecclesiastical individualism thus must be rejected.[15]

## Conclusion

We have examined a number of specific and practical examples that allow us to better understand *the limits of the obedience we owe to men*. These limits, as we have seen, are defined by the requirements of the Law-Word of God. We could bring forward many other questions—just as delicate and difficult—that would require very specific teaching from those whom God has established as instructors or teachers in His church in order to better understand the contemporary application of the teachings of Scripture. Such teaching would require believers to continue their growth in faith and to have a deeper unity with the church in Jesus Christ, a more fervent and united prayer of believers toward God. For the question that is posed here is one of belonging: are we, *as living phylacteries*, fully attached to God, faithfully submitted to our King, the unique Son, our Lord Jesus Christ, thus bearing the divine sign of His Word on our forehead (our thoughts), our hands (our actions), and our homes (our institutions)? For this sign commits us to obey the commands of God's Word, of God's Law, in every area of our lives. Or are we those who are content to merely listen to but who do not put into practice what they have heard and who, desiring no more of the gospel than the salvation of their souls, refuse the obedience demanded by the gospel of the kingdom of God? For the gospel of the kingdom of God leads us by faith to tear down the strongholds that men by their false reasoning set up against God, and then to bring to Him, from every nation of the earth, a people who fear and obey Him in all things.

If we refuse this obedience, if, to the Word of God—God's authority over every aspect of our life—we prefer our fallible traditions of men and churches and thus, separated from the true tradition of the apostles, we spurn sanctification, it will inevitably follow that we will place ourselves among those who will voluntarily deprive ourselves of the eternal presence of God. If we are rootless

---

[15] The subject of the exercise of authority within the church will be discussed further on. See the brilliant analysis of this kind of ecclesiastical individualism by Frédéric de Rougemont (trans. Colin Wright), *The Individualists in Church and State* (Wordbridge, Aalten, 2018).

Christians, if we are those who have not clothed ourselves with Jesus Christ and His righteousness, we will without fail take instead the mark and number of the beast: lies, injustice, and illusions. Because we did not desire to obey God rather than the man of sin, we will be helplessly delivered over to this beast mentioned in Revelation, to a state which claims sovereignty for itself, which makes itself god, which even places itself above God, which is a law to itself and thus overthrows the eternal Law of God. These, Scripture tells us, will have no part in the glorious kingdom of our Lord Jesus Christ.

ELEVEN

# Two Types of Power: the Magistrate and the Church

The institutional power of God manifests itself in two ways on earth: through the physical sword of the magistrate, the instrument of the state, and through the spiritual sword of the Word of God, wielded by the church of God.

**Both come from God**

The centurion in Matthew 8 said to Jesus, "Lord, I am not worthy that thou shouldest come under my roof: but speak the word only, and my servant shall be healed. For I am a man under authority, having soldiers under me: and I say to this man, Go, and he goeth; and to another, Come, and he cometh; and to my servant, Do this, and he doeth it" (Matt. 8:8-9).

We see here that there are two aspects to God's working among men: one quite human and the other divine. If, as the centurion tells us, his temporal earthly power comes from God—for indeed all power comes from God—and if it is through this divinely-ordained power that he is obeyed by his subordinates, then Jesus, possessing a divine power, will be all the more obeyed by His own spiritual servants, the angels, since He is God made man. Jesus therefore does not need to act directly Himself. He can simply issue orders to His angels, who will work wherever the Lord sends them.

Let's look at another example. To Pilate, Jesus declared that He was a King. But He added that His kingdom wasn't of this world, saying: "My kingdom is not of this world: if my kingdom were of this world, then would my servants fight, that I should not be delivered to the Jews: but now is my kingdom not from hence" (John 18:36).

Jesus has the heavenly army under His command, with whom He will judge the living and the dead. This will be the full and complete manifestation of His reign. When Peter, at the time of Jesus' arrest, drew his sword and cut off the ear of the high priest's servant, Jesus said to him: "Thinkest thou that I cannot now pray to my Father, and he shall presently give me more than twelve legions of angels?" (Matt. 26:53).

It was indeed this power of Jesus Christ over His heavenly servants that the centurion understood so well. He himself had soldiers under his command, which implies that he did not need to do a thing himself to make it happen; all he had to do was give an order to a soldier or servant. He could clearly see that Jesus, though on a different plane, was in a similar situation and therefore possessed a power similar to his own over His own spiritual servants. He had no need to personally move to heal the centurion's servant, for He too could give an order to an angel—utter a word—and the thing would be done. It is because of this most remarkable spiritual insight that Jesus affirms that He had never found such great faith in anyone in Israel (Matt. 8:10). T. Robert Ingram explains Jesus' astonished exclamation as follows:

> The marvel of the soldier's insight was that he saw not only the *nature* of authority as resting in the spoken word, but also that he understood the *seat* of authority in this world was divided. His own power was that of a soldier and the obedience [to] his word of command was connected with his power to kill. But he saw the same capacity to command in Jesus and recognized it as lying above and beyond his own as an army officer: Jesus, he saw, has power even over sin, sickness and death. Yet the power of the soldier was a reflection of the same authority with which Jesus had preached from the mountain; for, he said, I also am a man under authority. But while he could command soldiers, he could not command the forces of life. He appealed to Jesus's non-military power as superior to his own and independent of it, yet possessing the same ultimate nature. Truly his faith and insight was marvelous.[1]

---

[1] T. Robert Ingram, *The Two Powers* (St. Thomas Press, Houston, 1959), 4-5.

**These two powers have different roles which must not be confounded**

The Jews of Jesus' day never ceased to confuse these two powers. This is also often seen in His disciples who were so slow to understand the meaning and scope of the good news of the kingdom of God. This is visible in the incident we just mentioned where Peter drew his sword to defend his Master. Jesus, after healing the high priest's servant whose ear Peter cut off, said to him: "Put up again thy sword into his place: for all they that take the sword shall perish with the sword" (Matt. 26:52).

This is not a denial of the power of the sword. The magistrate has received from God the right, in certain cases defined by the Law, to take the life of evildoers.[2] Jesus rebukes Peter to show that he does not possess the authority of justice. It is not for the church to exercise the power of life and death that God has entrusted to the magistrate. This statement holds true even when this power or authority is that of the beast. At all times, Christians are exhorted to exercise the patience and faith of the saints, not accepting any compromise with the misguided state (being led "into captivity") yet also not seeking to overthrow this iniquitous power through revolution ("killing with the sword"). "He that leadeth into captivity shall go into captivity: he that killeth with the sword must be killed with the sword" (Rev. 13:10).[3]

What these texts condemn is not the temporal power's lawful use of the sword intended by God—which includes the death penalty—but the carnal revolutionary and seditious struggle of God's children who abandon their own spiritual jurisdiction to usurp the exercise of temporal power.

We can characterize the difference between the spiritual power of the church and the temporal power of the state as follows:

*The church* (in this world) manifests the ministry of grace,

---

[2] Despite the contrary opinion of many Christians, the death penalty is legitimized by the Bible. On this subject see T. Robert Ingram, ed., *Essays on the Death Penalty* (St. Thomas Press, Houston, 1978), which includes the celebrated essay by C. S. Lewis; A. R. Kayayan, *Pénologie: Considérations chrétiennes sur la peine de mort* (Perspectives Réformées, Palos Heights, 1993); R. L. Bruckberger, *Oui à la peine de mort* (Plon, Paris, 1985); Edward Feser and Joseph M. Bessette, *By Man Shall His Blood Be Shed: A Catholic Defense of Capital Punishment* (Ignatius Press, San Francisco, 2018).

[3] This passage can be more appropriately interpreted as indicating the inevitable retributive divine judgment on those who imprison Christians ("leadeth into captivity") and on those who martyr Christians ("killeth with the sword").

the ministry of God's mercy. Through her working throughout history, she reveals the time of God's patience and longsuffering (Rom. 2:4). For Christ at His incarnation did not come to judge the world. God does not desire the death of the sinner but rather his repentance, that he might have eternal life and escape the Judgment (John 5:24). "The Lord is . . . longsuffering to us-ward, not willing that any should perish, but that all should come to repentance" (2 Pet. 3:9).

God's judgment and vengeance do not belong to the church at present. It is only when the Lord returns in glory that the saints will also be clothed—in Christ—with this power (Matt. 19:28; Rom. 16:20).

But the function of *the magistrate* is wholly different. His power also comes from God, but it is a temporal power. Civil power exercises the power of the sword to restrain evil. The ministry of the sword is a foreshadowing of the last judgment.

The disciples had a difficult time understanding that Christ had come as a servant; that the greatness of the citizen of the kingdom was measured on an absolutely different scale than that of the subjects of the ruler of this world; that in the kingdom of God he who wishes to be greatest must make himself the lowliest; that in order to rule with Christ we must, just like Christ, be the servant of all. And, finally, that it is by faithfulness to God's least commandments that true greatness in the kingdom is measured: "Whosoever therefore shall break one of these least commandments, and shall teach men so, he shall be called the least in the kingdom of heaven" (Matt. 5:19).

The disciples' difficulty of understanding the true greatness of the kingdom of God is remarkably illustrated in Luke 22:24-26:

> And there was also a strife among them, which of them should be accounted the greatest. And he said unto them, The kings of the Gentiles exercise lordship over them; and they that exercise authority upon them are called benefactors. But ye shall not be so: but he that is greatest among you, let him be as the younger; and he that is chief, as he that doth serve.

Not for a single moment did Jesus challenge the civil power, "the kings of the Gentiles," or their right to "exercise lordship over" the people under their authority or to exercise the harsh power of the sword over them. On the contrary, He says that those who do so—that is, those who govern as masters or rulers—are called "benefactors" by their subjects because, by the fact that they govern (even if their authority is a harsh and ruthless power), they always restrain the utterly destructive forces of social anarchy.

But Christ tells His disciples that power in the church must not be exercised in this way, for the church's power is the visible manifestation of the authority that Christ as a Husband exercises over His church through the working of the Holy Spirit. It is this spirit of goodness (not the harsh sword of the magistrate) that, according to the Word of God, must reign in the church of God. It is through this power of God, acting through the weakness of the man crucified in Christ, that the church of the living God must be governed.

## TWELVE

# The Nature of Power within the Local Church

It is in the weakness of the flesh (and through the power of the Holy Spirit) that power is exercised by those whom God has placed in His church to govern. It is in this weakness that the apostles, prophets, evangelists, pastors and teachers, deacons, elders, and other servants of God must exercise the ministry which the Holy Spirit has entrusted to them for the building up of the body of Christ, the church of the living God. This is why the Apostle Peter, after receiving from Christ the order to feed His sheep, wrote:

> Feed the flock of God which is among you, taking the oversight thereof, not by constraint, but willingly; not for filthy lucre, but of a ready mind; neither as being lords over God's heritage, but being examples to the flock. (1 Pet. 5:2-3)

When the Apostle Paul addressed the Philippians, and particularly their spiritual leaders, he exhorted them to imitate the way the Lord Jesus Christ had exercised the power entrusted to Him by His Father in His earthly ministry:

> Let this mind be in you, which was also in Christ Jesus: who, being in the form of God, thought it not robbery to be equal with God: but made himself of no reputation, and took upon him the form of a servant, and was made in the likeness of men. (Phil. 2:5-7)

This exhortation echoed the words of Jesus Himself who said to His disciples: "For whether is greater, he that sitteth at meat, or he that serveth? is not he that sitteth at meat? but I am among you as he that serveth" (Luke 22:27).

We see, therefore, that a true pastor does not act toward the flock entrusted to him by the Great Shepherd of the sheep as does the civil power: by coercion, by a domination marked by force. (We must remember that the physical force of the sword exercised by the magistrate is perfectly legitimate when applied in its proper order—that is, of course, as long as it remains under the yoke of God's Law.) No, the servant of God acts as crucified with Jesus Christ, in complete weakness, through the power of the Holy Spirit—a divine power indeed, but not one which violently coerces or compels people. The true servant of God must constantly remember these words of the prophet Zechariah while living and revealing the true significance of his ministry: "Not by might, nor by power [will this work be accomplished], but by My Spirit, saith the LORD of hosts" (Zech. 4:6).

Therefore, the weaker the power of true spiritual leaders is (humanly speaking), so much more must believers be subject to this power and humbly obedient to it. Thus the Apostle Paul, aware that the exercise of his ministry was to be carried out in man's weakness, said, "death worketh in us, but life in you" (2 Cor. 4:6).

Fully convinced that the only position faithful to Christ's teaching is that of crucifixion, the apostle exhorts believers in this way:

> Obey them that have the rule over you, and submit yourselves: for they watch for your souls, as they that must give account, that they may do it with joy, and not with grief: for that is unprofitable for you. (Heb. 13:17)

This power is all the more powerful, being the power that the Father has given to the Son, acting through the Third Person of the Godhead, the Holy Spirit, as He labors in the weakness of men chosen by God for this task. The less this ministry possesses of human power, the less "political" force it holds, the more unwise it is for Christians placed beneath its authority to disobey it. For the church holds in earthen vessels the power of Christ to open or close the door of the kingdom of God and even to deliver hardened rebels to Satan.

But it is also essential to clearly state: this obedience of Christians to the authority of the church must always be maintained according to the analogy of Faith. That is, the obedience of God's children to the power that Christ has placed in His church must never be a blind, unconditional, purely mechanical obedience. Just as the shepherds must watch over the flock so that the sheep may walk in obedience to the truth, so also the members of the spiritual community must watch over the shepherds whom God has placed over them, in order that they might verify that these leaders of the church also submit to the commands of Scripture. Church members must watch over their shepherds just as Paul's Jewish listeners did in the city of Berea. "They received the word with all readiness of mind, and searched the scriptures daily, whether those things were so" (Acts 17:11).

We are not required to obey ecclesiastical orders contrary to the commands of God's written revelation. For the Bible does not require us to submit to the human traditions of churches but to the Word of Truth, to Sacred Scripture, which is the true tradition of the apostles.

**Is the exercise of power in the local church monarchical, aristocratic, or democratic?**

According to Holy Scripture, the exercise of power in the church is monarchical, aristocratic, and democratic *all at the same time.*

It is *monarchical* because the sole head of the church (possessing an absolutely sovereign power over it) is Jesus Christ Himself, God the Son made man. In this way we must first affirm that the church is an institution with a theocentric, theonomic, and theocratic character, and that the prerogative that governs the church is the prerogative of God, the very Word of God. The life of the church is nothing more than the obedience of believers, through the faith and power given to them by the Holy Spirit, to all the orders of their Head and Leader, their King Jesus Christ, which orders are contained in the Bible.

But we must immediately add that the earthly government of the church is of an *aristocratic* or *hierarchical* nature, for the Head of the church, Jesus Christ, appoints men specifically chosen and trained by Him and to whom He has delegated His authority to govern His house according to the commandments included for this explicit purpose in the Word of God. The ministers of God in the church are thus in no way instituted by popular election, by the democratic vote of all believers, but by God Himself.

> And God hath set some in the church, first apostles, secondarily prophets, thirdly teachers, . . . (1 Cor. 12:28)

> And I thank Christ Jesus our Lord, who hath enabled me, for that he counted me faithful, putting me into the ministry. (1 Tim. 1:12)

> Paul, an apostle, not of men, neither by man, but by Jesus Christ, and God the Father . . . (Gal. 1:1)

These ministers, these servants of God, are chosen by God from among the "faithful," the "made men" of the church, and have the task of governing it in such a way that it is the Lord Jesus Christ Himself who builds it up through His Spirit. They are instituted by God and not by the Christian "people" who, at most, only recognize their calling and confirm them in their charge. Nothing is more contrary to Scripture than to believe that the church should be ruled by the opinions and decisions of the majority of its members (as is the case with any liberal democratic society)—that is, independent or "free" from the constraints and limits of the Law of God.

But we must simultaneously add that the church is also a society of a *democratic* nature, a society of people capable of mutual edification, a community in which all are, in their own right, members of the body of Jesus Christ. Paul writes to the Christians at Rome that he desires to see them so that he might impart to them some spiritual gift, that they might be strengthened (Rom. 1:11). Such a concern to do good to the Christian people of the city of Rome was just and legitimate. For he whom Jesus Christ had established as the apostle of the nations had received from God the power to strengthen believers and to communicate to them the graces that God would see fit to grant them. But Paul catches himself, for he realizes that these believers can also be used by God for his own strengthening. This is why he immediately adds: "that is, that I may be comforted together with you by the mutual faith both of you and me" (Rom. 1:12).

This faith of God's people, writes Peter, is a faith just as precious and valuable as his own (2 Pet. 1:1). It is from this communion of all in one body, where every person has his own place, that democracy exists in the church in accordance with Scripture.

In Christ, through the Holy Spirit, in this community which is the body of Christ, this heavenly Jerusalem that we already live in by faith, all members are useful, all have their place, and none should be despised, set aside, or ignored.

> For ye are all the children of God by faith in Christ Jesus. For as many of you as have been baptized into Christ have put on Christ. There is neither Jew nor Greek, there is neither bond nor free, there is neither male nor female: for ye are all one in Christ Jesus. (Gal. 3:26-28; see also Col. 3:11 and 1 Cor. 12:13)

We are all prophets, priests, and kings in Jesus Christ. The Holy Spirit, who blows where He chooses, works indiscriminately among people both through the most modest members of the body of Christ as well as through those whom God has established as pastors and teachers in His church. If the ministers of Jesus Christ must labor in the teaching and building up of the church of God, believers also have an indispensable role to play, for they must ensure that the teaching, edification, and government of the church are carried out according to the "measure of faith" (Rom. 12:6) in the one Truth, in accordance with the deposit given once for all to the saints in the Holy Scriptures.

At a time when the "teachers" of the church are all too frequently merely false teachers dispensing false and harmful doctrine, God often uses the faith of the humblest believer to keep His church alive and to defend it from error, the lies of the devil.

**Discipline within the church**

The exercise of this power in the church through the consistorial authority of the elders can lead to acts of discipline that culminate in the exclusion of the hardened wrongdoer from the fellowship of Christians in the hope that this spiritual and social isolation might lead him to reflection, questioning, and repentance. The power of the church cannot proceed beyond the exclusion of those who, through their actions or teaching, abandon the rule of Faith and work toward the destruction of the Christian community. Scripture clearly teaches that, after various warnings given to the brother who professes the error or who behaves contrary to the teachings of the apostles, if he perseveres in his error or misbehavior, the believers who constitute the church must absolutely separate themselves from him. In fact, it is the unfaithful professing Christian who, by his persistence in his errors, himself breaks the bond of fellowship. The church merely recognizes this and acts in consequence. This separation from the unfaithful sheep is a sign of God's disapproval of the person who, while professing to be a Christian, perseveres in wrongdoing; it seeks to protect the flock from any contagion and in the end to work, as far as possible, toward the repentance and eventual restoration of the unruly brother. Separation, the isolation of one who is thus abandoned by all, should lead him to repentance, reparation, and reintegration into the people of God.

The only method of discipline applicable in the church of God is that described in Leviticus for lepers (Lev. 13:1-46): a scrupulous examination of each case by the priests and a separation from the infected person if the disease turns out to be leprosy. In the event of recovery, the presumed healed patient is again to be carefully examined by the priests and his reintegration publicly proclaimed if his recovery is confirmed. Thus the house of God does not participate in the uncleanness of the lepers. The same is true of heresy or persistent immorality, which are moral and spiritual impurities that must not be permitted to contaminate or pollute the church of God. We must defend the church's mark of holiness: "I believe in one holy, catholic, and apostolic church."

We must resolutely exclude the hardened sinner or heretic from the very bosom of the church of God. However, the retributive power of the church can proceed no further than this. To ask the civil power to deprive this sheep of its life, liberty, or property because of heresy or lasting immorality is in fact to usurp the place of Christ and to arrogate today the authority of the final judgment, a privilege that belongs exclusively to God.[1] It is clear that this ecclesiastical discipline cannot destroy creational family ties, either.

---

[1] See, among other passages, Matthew 18:15-17, 1 Corinthians 5:6-13, and 2 Thessalonians 3:6.

It was this disciplinary power *in the church* that Christ exercised when He drove the sellers and money changers out of the temple.

**Is a woman's submission to the authority God has given to man harmful to her spiritual life in the church?**[2]

In Christ, writes the Apostle Paul, there is neither male nor female, slave nor free, Jew nor Gentile (Col. 3:11). According to this text, the new man is he who continually renews himself after the image of the One who created him. It is Christ who is all and in all, and of whom all the children of God are members. This text, which attests to the universal royal priesthood of all believers irrespective of age, social rank, ethnicity, or sex, has been used to establish absolute equality within the church and to abolish the authority established by God of man over woman and master over his servants or slaves. Jesus Christ answered this question when He revealed that, at the resurrection when He will indeed be all and in all, there will be no flesh or blood (1 Cor. 15:50). Our bodies will then be gloriously resurrected, incorruptible, full of power (1 Cor. 15:43-44). We will no longer marry, and the resurrected will be like the angels in heaven (Matt. 22:30). Of this state of perfect unity and liberty in Christ, we today possess only the firstfruits of the Spirit (Rom. 8:23). The resurrection of the body has not yet taken place, and we still await the adoption, the redemption of our bodies (Rom. 8:23; 2 Tim. 2:18). Thus, as new creatures, we live by the Spirit in the liberty of the children of God, of which we enjoy the firstfruits; and, at the same time, we live in flesh and blood, in our body and earthly psyche, subject to the conditions of the good earthly life that God has given us.

These considerations lead us to examine the position of the Christian woman in the church in two distinct but inseparable aspects. Indeed, they are as inseparable as are the divine and human nature in the single Person of Jesus Christ, Son of God and Son of Man, like unto us in everything but sin.

Let us first consider woman's condition within the church in relation to the limits of her human nature and then according to

---

[2] On this important question, see the following works: Stephen B. Clark, *Man and Woman in Christ;* John Piper and Wayne Grudem, *Recovering Biblical Manhood and Womanhood.* See also Benjamin B. Warfield, Robert L. Dabney, and Geoffrey Thomas, *Women Speaking in the Church: What does the Scripture Say?* (Solid Ground Christian Books, Birmingham, Alabama, 2014).

her submission to the special constraints imposed on her by sin. On this subject Paul writes very explicitly that he does not allow women "to teach, nor to usurp authority over the man," but instead vigorously exhorts them to remain in submission (1 Tim. 2:12). And, in this same epistle to Timothy, he also writes that he who aspires to be an elder must govern his own house well. Thus we see that the condition of woman as a woman forbids her any function in which she would manifest any authority over man, and more specifically to aspire to the charge of teaching men.

On the other hand, the apostle strongly encourages her to take on the task of teaching children. More than that, she has the duty, if she possesses the qualifications, of teaching other women younger than herself about their domestic duties and how women should carry out the duties of the Christian life. For, in order to raise children, aren't both parents required to exercise authority over them and instruct them? And aren't the elder women in the church told that they must instruct the younger women to love their husbands and children, to be chaste, modest, occupied in their homes and, finally, to be subject to their husbands so that the Word of God might not be exposed to any shame (Tit. 2:4-5)? Didn't Paul expressly issue an order that young widows should remarry and have children and manage their own house (1 Tim. 5:14), which sometimes involves commanding, taking authority over servants and maids and over male and female slaves? For, if the power exercised by the woman over her immediate surroundings comes from her position as mistress of the household, she can indeed exercise the very authority of her husband himself (by delegation) during his absence.

Thus, in the church, the ministry of authority can never be that of a woman.[3] In fact, the teaching of the New Testament, as well as the practice of the Christian communities there described to us, shows us that the ministry of authority within the church is reserved for those who are:

1. Converts
2. Men
3. Accomplished men, with authority over their own

---

[3] We would here add that the tendency in today's world to grant more and more authority to women is in opposition to God's clear purposes in every aspect of life and not only in the church.

homes, *and*
4. Men given by Christ to the church for this specific task[4]

As a believer, the Christian woman (and the man as well, for that matter!) is perfectly complete in Jesus Christ (Col. 2:10). Despite her natural weakness and her necessary submission to man, she is with him a full heir to the grace of life (1 Pet. 3:7). All who remain in Christ are equally prophets, priests, and kings in Jesus Christ, whether they are male or female (Ex. 19:6; Rom. 12:1; 1 Pet. 2:5, 9; Rev. 1:6; 19:10). The Spirit blows where He wills and does not concern Himself about earthly distinctions between believers. He acts wherever He pleases. Joel 2:28-32 declares this, a text whose fulfillment manifested itself in the coming of the Holy Spirit at Pentecost. Since that time, the Holy Spirit has been spread over all without distinction. All, men and women, sons and daughters, young people and elderly, slave and free, are therefore partakers of the blessing of all the graces and anointing with which the Holy Spirit will enrich them (Acts 2:14-21). Thus, though the woman does not possess the right to teach in the congregation or to assume authority over any man, she can and may pray both in private and in public prayer meetings, as all God's children must do, and be available to receive, express, and transmit in all modesty to others the graces that God will give her for the edification of the church, while always carefully refraining from taking a position of dominion over man and thus seeking, through her pride, to steal from God the glory that belongs to Him alone.

---

[4] These ministries are given to the church militant to assist the saints to attain to the perfect stature of Christ (Eph. 4:13). When perfection has come (1 Cor. 13:10) at the resurrection of the dead, what was necessary for the perfecting of the saints will no longer be required, which shows that the ministries which are necessary for the embattled church, the church militant in the process of perfection, will no longer have a place in the church triumphant, when Christ will be all and in all.

THIRTEEN

# How Can a Christian Exercise Such Power?

By the Holy Spirit who dwells in him through faith, *a Christian has power over himself.* He can exercise this self-control, this mastery of his soul and body which the Apostle Peter speaks of (2 Pet. 1:6; cf. Gal. 5:22-23). Any abdication of this power of the Holy Spirit over the sinful impulses of the flesh can only grieve the Spirit of God in the Christian and must necessarily lead to all the disorders of body and soul. It is this discipline that the Christian exercises over himself (with the help of the Holy Spirit in him) that allows him to submit the desires of his soul and body to God's will—that is, to God's Law. His aim is to conform his entire person to the image of Jesus Christ. This is the indispensable foundation for the exercise of all Christian authority. Since this authority comes from God, since it is a fruit of the Holy Spirit, and since Christ opened for us the way into all the blessings of God if we obey His commandments, let us be assured that He will grant us His strength to exercise the power He expects of us in whatever situation He places before us. The exercise of this divine power is in fact a victory over the forces of Satan, the flesh, and the world; and this victory is assured if we remain firmly rooted in Jesus Christ.

Our battle therefore is not against "flesh and blood"—that is, against *body* and *soul,* our physical life and being.[1] For the whole man, both body and soul, was created perfectly good, fell into sin, and in Christ is entirely recreated by God in the image of His Son. Our battle, says the Apostle Paul, is against the principalities, powers, and evil spirits in the heavenly places. Thus *the struggle against*

---

[1] On the necessary distinction (not opposition) of the soul and body within a single individual, see John W. Cooper, *Body, Soul and Life Everlasting: Biblical Anthropology and the Monism-Dualism Debate* (Regent College Publishing, Vancouver, 1995).

*the flesh* which Scripture so insistently speaks about is nothing more than the struggle we wage, by the strength given us through the Holy Spirit, against the power of the Evil One acting on the flesh, the principle of sin in us. It is this fleshly principle which so easily dominates our body and soul. Paul urges us not to give in to the body's lusts—passion, softness, the love of comfort, the undue aspiration to sensual and spiritual pleasure. These self-centered carnal pleasures—both of soul and body—are not joys given by God in a well-structured emotional sensibility but are instead various forms of chaos within the senses. Rather, Scripture constantly exhorts us to master these evil impulses through the sanctified exercise of our will, now renewed by the Holy Spirit. Neither the body nor the soul, nor the emotions nor the mind, are evil of themselves; instead, it is the sinful impulses of our body and soul that must be victoriously rejected by us, being firmly rooted and grounded in Christ's victory at the Cross:

> Submit yourselves therefore to God. Resist the devil, and he will flee from you. Draw nigh to God, and he will draw nigh to you. Cleanse your hands, ye sinners; and purify your hearts, ye double minded. (Jas. 4:7-8)

**The exercise of power over those God has placed under our authority**

By the Holy Spirit who reigns in him, the Christian husband and father has power over his own family. Indeed, according to Scripture, his *wife* owes him obedience just as the church owes it to Jesus Christ (Eph. 5:22-33). *Children* must obey their parents just as they must obey their Heavenly Father because these parents are a tangible image of the Father. Scripture says it quite clearly: it is from the Heavenly Father that every family (*patria* in Greek) in heaven and on earth derives its name (Eph. 3:14-15). Thus, any rebellion of the Christian wife against the authority of her husband is a challenge and defiance to the Lord Jesus Christ Himself. Similarly, any rebellion of children against the authority of their parents is a revolt against the Father, against God Himself. Since the power of the Christian husband and parents is exercised through the strength of the Holy Spirit, this power must be exercised in a manner analogous to that exercised by the Lord Jesus Christ over His church. That is, just as Christ did for His church, so the husband (in relation to his wife) and both parents (in relation to their children) must love those over whom God has placed them in authority even to the sacrifice of their lives. Thus, parents must exercise authority over their children in the same way that the Heavenly Father does, in peace, gentleness, and firmness, sparing them neither love nor punishment, so that they might not become embittered or dissolute. For, in a Christian family, the parents exercise both the power of the magistrate (to punish and praise) and that of the church (to bless and to pave the way to the kingdom of God). As a result, they must never spare their children (as needed) from the exercise of the rod or the practice of prayer.

Similarly, the authority a *master* exercises over his servants and slaves comes from God. Likewise, the authority of an *employer* over his employees is entrusted to him by God. The same is also true of an officer over his soldiers or a manager over his personnel. On the other hand, any rebellion, any fraud of the employee (Christian or non-Christian) toward his employer is, in the end, nothing less than a defiance launched in the face of his Heavenly Employer.[2] Scripture tells us that we must pray by lifting up pure hands to heaven, without wrath or doubting (1 Tim. 2:8).

The Christian employer, in exercising his authority over his workers, must remember that he too has a Master in heaven, and it is to this Heavenly Master that he will one day be held accountable for all his actions. This is likewise true of an officer (either in the police or the armed forces) over his subordinates.

**Difficulties in the exercise of power**

If we are unable to exercise the power that God expects of us, the fault is probably with us in the first place and not with those who refuse to submit in the Lord to the authority entrusted to us. Thus, if a Christian wife, child, or employee refuses obedience and submission, the husband, father, and Christian employer must first examine his own heart in an attempt to discover what might be pre-

---

[2] Here it would be quite beneficial to examine the illegitimate labor and employer violence exercised both by trade union pressures and by the arbitrary price and wage fixing by monopolies between holders of capital. Union tyranny is no better than employer tyranny except for the fact that the former has the exacerbating element that it overthrows the authority established by God. Even unions themselves must also submit to the requirements of God's Law.

venting the Holy Spirit from exercising the sovereign power of Jesus Christ through him. It is only after this act of personal examination and internal cleansing, repentance, and renewed obedience that he will be able to act effectively toward the sins of his loved ones. This is the biblical principle of the mote and the beam (Matt. 7:1-5). This is why God does not allow a potential deacon, bishop, or elder to exercise power over the house of God if he doesn't first know how to be obeyed by his wife and children. Moreover, experience clearly shows that if a pastor cannot be obeyed by his wife and children, his preaching and his works won't be able to manifest the power of God for the instruction, edification, and sanctification of his flock.

On the other hand, the difficult predispositions, bad character, injustice, wickedness, or spinelessness of the husband, parents, master, or boss in no way exempt believers who are subject to their authority from rendering them the honor, respect, submission, and obedience they owe them. Though we must always refuse to commit the sins that such superiors might impose on us, we cannot escape through our revolt or rebellion from the injustices that these same superiors might inflict on us. It is here that we must daily learn to bear our cross, obeying (in a non-selective way!) all the demands of the Word of God.

It is here too that we must in all things depend on the Comforter, the Holy Spirit, and that we must learn to exercise this faith which must move the mountains of our daily lives. This is where we must take care *not to abandon the faith*. We must examine ourselves to know whether we are indeed in the faith (2 Cor. 13:5). For, by trying to change our circumstances through purely carnal efforts, we too often seek to escape from this cross that (if we are true Christians) we must bear every day. It is also here that we must exercise this unfailing patience that characterizes the mature Christian, a patience that must not give in to bitterness, backbiting, rebellion, or grumbling dissent. None of these attitudes (let alone the actions they produce) can work toward the building up of the kingdom of God. For it is here that the patience and faith of the saints is revealed (Rev. 13:10). Patience and faith which are neither passive resignation nor open rebellion, nor obedience to injustice nor disobedience to God, but the very power of God who, through our weakness, deploys His heavenly strength in the victory He wins in us and through us over the world.

This is also where we see the diabolical side of rebellion and the illegitimate challenge against any authority that proceeds from God.[3] Let us note: woman's desire for egalitarian independence and her often subtle aspiration to seize authority in marriage, to dominate over her husband and to rule him; children's rebellion and their challenging of the authority of their parents; the spirit of dispute, quarrelsomeness, union and social pressure leading to the use of force by the employee to fight injustice or to satisfy his material lust—mob actions that have often yielded to the inherently pathological dialectical ideology of class struggle—are to be condemned as so many sinful temptations. The created order is one of peace within work, harmony of classes, sexes, and generations.

On the other hand, class struggle and the battle between races, nations, ethnicities, sexes, generations, etc., are pathological phenomena that cannot in any way produce good. This does not mean, however, that men, women, children, people of various colors, nations or ethnicities, or the working class are never the objects of injustice (especially on the part of social or territorial superiors) and that such injustices should not be redressed. It should be added that in a properly hierarchical society, healthy secondary authorities can (and must) play an important legitimate role in the redressing of societal injustices. But the way of this recovery will not be through a challenge to existing authority nor through a desire to destroy the institution which is operating unjustly. For the desire to redress injustices through revolution—itself unjust—forgets that any violation (even a humanly understandable violation) of God's Law can only increase the mass of injustice that destroys society. This unbelieving attitude also forgets the working of God's providence which, in His sovereign and all-powerful action, can respond to the prayers of those who trust in Him and thus turn evil into good. If man seeks first the kingdom of God and His righteousness, will his Heavenly Father—who cares for even the smallest of birds—fail to give him, above all, all that he needs?

We see that Christians' participation in revolutionary movements, as well as in class struggle or in the struggle between gen-

---

[3] "My son, fear thou the LORD and the king: and meddle not with them that are given to change: for their calamity shall rise suddenly; and who knoweth the ruin of them both?" (Prov. 24:21-22). "I will therefore that men pray every where, lifting up holy hands, without wrath and doubting" (1 Tim. 2:8).

erations, ethnicities, or sexes, merely reveals the spirit of injustice that animates them as well as their (often unconscious) rejection of the Law of God.[4] The Christian's search for personal and social justice must first proceed from his own transformation, an inner change that will allow him to act justly in the various spheres of his own life. Only then will he be able to act in a beneficial way (without harmful side effects) on the institutions over which he has been granted responsibility. We also see how all the liberal, socialist, economic, utopian, Jacobin, and messianic revolutions—red, pink, brown, black, white, orange, or green of the past centuries—are all signs of the growing activity in our world of the divider (*diabolos*), the adversary, this Satan and his angels that Christ has left for a time to act like the prince of this world.

The change that God desires to see taking place in an unjust

---

[4] What we say here must not in any way be construed as justifying the abuses of power and the injustices committed by those who hold positions of authority in the workplace. Seeking justice (conformity to God's Law) within a company is quite different from exacerbating class struggle, the social conflicts so often advocated by trade unionists as the only way to resolve social injustices. Let us simply remember that when the Marxists seize political power, all freedom of association disappears. It should be added that for the Marxists, trade union struggles are much more a useful means of seizing power than of redressing genuine injustices. The revolutionary aggression against private property and against all forms of capitalism (except, of course, the benevolent monopoly of the monopolistic capitalism of the communist state!) is not an attack on the *abuses* of these created institutions but is rather an attack *on their very existence*, an attack diametrically opposed to the Law of God that protects property and private capital (see the eighth and tenth commandment and Exodus 20:15-17), and against God Himself. This is evidenced by the following excerpt from a letter addressed by the Brazilian revolutionary bishop Helder Camara to the French political philosopher Roger Garaudy, at the time the instigator of a Marxist Christianity: "The next step for us Christians to accomplish is to publicly proclaim that it is not socialism but capitalism that is inherently perverse, and that socialism is only reprehensible in its perversions" (Roger Garaudy, *Parole d'Homme*, Laffont, Paris, p. 118).

This assertion is the exact opposite of the truth. It is not private property that is reprehensible. The culprits here are, on the one hand, the unlimited accumulation of this property by the state—state collectivization—the erroneous purpose and conclusion of both socialism and communism; and, on the other hand, the accumulation of the wealth of many countries by capitalistic trusts whose economic power depends on monopolies granted by the state and by the fraudulent speculative methods of casino-type financial theft practiced on the stock exchange everywhere. This is especially true of the United States. See, among many others, John Perkins, *Confessions of an Economic Hit Man* (Berrett-Koehler Publishers, 2004); *New Confessions of an Economic Hit Man* (Ebury Press, 2018). See also Jean-Marc Berthoud, *Les Dix Commandements lus par la Bible: Une Lumière divine pour notre temps: Le huitième commandement*.

world is not first of all an external, formal change that leaves the root of sin within man intact. Let us repeat, such changes will in the long run merely consolidate the lasting nature of evil in society. But through a spiritual change, through an act of new creation in man, through our regeneration in Jesus Christ, God will work, through His children's ever-increasing obedience to His commandments in every area of life, to the restoration of all things, to the gathering of all aspects of life in Jesus Christ. It is in this way that a true institutional restoration of society, according to the created order of the Law-Word of God, will be possible.

FOURTEEN

# Why Does God Require Such Relationships of Hierarchy and Subordination?

Why is it that these relationships of hierarchy and subordination exist? Why does God demand such relationships of power and subordination, of authority and submission, of commandment and obedience to Christ from His children and all mankind? Aren't we free in Christ? Doesn't the Apostle Paul tell us that in Christ there are no more slaves, masters, female or male, young or old, Jew or Gentile? So why does this hierarchical order still exist?

    We must not forget that it is through the Spirit that we dwell in the kingdom of God where this freedom reigns. But we must also remember that at present this Spirit dwells within our body and soul, and as a result He reigns over this body and soul. That is, we live in the creation of God, a creation that—even before the appearance of sin—possessed order and hierarchy. But, since the fall, the hold of sin on our flesh has made these institutions even more important. Now more than ever we as sinful beings stand in need of such a submission to these salutary authorities instituted by God to assist us in our battle against the sin within us. What is even more serious for us Christians is the fact that if we do not put these sinful works to death in Christ, Satan and his angels can still act upon this flesh that we still allow to function within us. Even more, if we do not put this old fleshly man to death, if we do not resist Satan by the power of Christ within us, by obeying through the Spirit the commandments of God, we will allow the enemy to enjoy an even greater hold on our lives. If this complacency to sin continues to persist in the Christian, he merely reveals to the eyes of all that he does not truly belong to the kingdom of Christ.

Nor should we forget that our life as children of God is by no means this individualist pseudo-democracy (the meager glory of our Western world) nor this rational and ethical autonomy which is the very height of sin. Nor are we mere cogs in this totalitarian collectivist machine called social democratic technocracy. Nor did God create us to return to the nominalist and existentialist chaos of those who, driven by the syncretistic power of lies animated by Satan, despise the order of creation and labor to change its laws and times (Dan. 7:25). God created an order composed of men and women; and by the effect of His blessing, man and woman multiply and form families. By forming families, these men and women become clans, tribes, cities, and nations. This order—even before the fall—was subject to the Law of God, and this Law establishes a hierarchical harmony among mankind. It is by individually and publicly acknowledging this order and by voluntarily submitting to it that human community, according to God's desired pattern, will be restored. Sin is nothing but the violation of the divine clauses constituting this order, and Satan's goal is to constantly seek to divert people from obedience to that order, for it is an order of life, of blessed life in God. It is through obedience to the rules of this order—that is, to the divine Law that instituted it—that love for God and one's neighbor consist.[1]

> Ye shall therefore keep my statutes, and my judgments: which if a man do, he shall live in them: I am the LORD. (Lev. 18:5)

> For this commandment which I command thee this day, it is not hidden from thee, neither is it far off. . . . But the word is very nigh unto thee, in thy mouth, and in thy heart, that thou mayest do it. (Deut. 30:11-14)

It is for the protection of the life of our soul and body, for the protection of the life of human society, the family, the community, the nation, and creation that God has ordered us to live according to these hierarchical relationships of power and submission in conformity to the Law of God. He who, under the false pretext of human freedom or the "freedom" given by the Spirit, seeks to abolish these

---
[1] See Jean-Marc Berthoud, *Apologie pour la Loi de Dieu*.

safeguards given to us by God Himself for our good, is very likely to fall into a cherubic syndrome that delights in the dangerous illusion of his own natural innocence, a pernicious, murderous, and revolutionary naivety. This is no longer a question of the freedom given by the Holy Spirit, a divine freedom that is nothing but the ever-increasing conformity of our lives to the model of Jesus Christ and an ever-increasing desire within us to obey God's commandments. Rather, this is the "freedom" of the fallen angels, of the demons who attempt to lead us in revolt against the holy Law of God and against the order of creation. It is this false freedom of the flesh that libertinism claims to be true human freedom. Freedom according to God's definition is not the freedom to do what one wants—that is, to make a god of oneself, deciding for oneself what is right and wrong and thus usurping the place of the Creator, the divine Legislator. To the contrary, this is a picture of man in rebellion against God who reserves for himself the freedom to do evil. Such freedom against God—or, just as accurately, against ourselves, for (whether we like it or not) we are all created in the very image of the God we reject—is nothing but the freedom of self-destruction.

True freedom is to conform ourselves, through faith in Christ and the working of the Holy Spirit within us, to the Law of God, which is a figure of the perfect image of God, an image that we can contemplate in the divine and human Person of our Lord Jesus Christ. By obeying Christ in this way, through faith and regeneration and out of love for God and our neighbor, we will find our true nature, a new nature created in the image of Jesus Christ. Life is found only in this obedience by faith to God's commandments (Col. 3:10-11; Eph. 4:24).

This is why man, if he turns away from this hierarchical order that God has established for our good, will inevitably destroy himself; he will commit spiritual suicide; he will squander his physical and mental health; and he will be destroyed both socially and politically. The family and all social structures will become sources of endless evil and suffering for him. Thus, for those who refuse to conform their behavior to God's commandments, the blessing normally derived from the hierarchical order established by God is transformed into true curses. This is the law of the covenant of creation.

> And the LORD God took the man, and put him into the garden of Eden to dress it and to keep it. And the LORD God commanded the man, saying, Of every tree of the garden thou mayest freely eat: but of the tree of the knowledge of good and evil, thou shalt not eat of it: for in the day that thou eatest thereof thou shalt surely die. (Gen. 2:15-17)

This covenant is repeated in the following terms at the conclusion of the Torah:

> I call heaven and earth to record this day against you, that I have set before you life and death, blessing and cursing: therefore choose life, that both thou and thy seed may live: that thou mayest love the LORD thy God, and that thou mayest obey his voice, and that thou mayest cleave unto him: for he is thy life, and the length of thy days: that thou mayest dwell in the land which the LORD sware unto thy fathers, to Abraham, to Isaac, and to Jacob, to give them. (Deut. 30:19-20)

Nor does the New Covenant speak in any other way:

> Take heed, brethren, lest there be in any of you an evil heart of unbelief, in departing from the living God. But exhort one another daily, while it is called To day; lest any of you be hardened through the deceitfulness of sin. For we are made partakers of Christ, if we hold the beginning of our confidence stedfast unto the end; while it is said, To day if ye will hear his voice, harden not your hearts, as in the provocation. (Heb. 3:12-15)

FIFTEEN

# What Does the Necessary Separation of Powers Mean?

It is right to distinguish and even to *separate*—though not to *oppose*—temporal and spiritual powers. Spiritual power, the church of God, is led by Jesus Christ and has a duty to conform to the normative and obligatory teachings of God's Word pertaining to it. The same is true of temporal power with regards to what pertains to it. The magistrate—the public service of what we call the "state"—also has Christ as its leader and must also conform itself (in matters of temporal power) to God's Law, for it must punish evildoers and favor the good (Rom. 13:1-7). For, though the magistrate holds his power directly from God and not through the delegation of the church (as claimed by the imperial papacy of the High Middle Ages—at least since Popes Gregory VII, Innocent III, and Boniface VIII), yet this power must be exercised under the final authority of God—that is, in conformity to the appropriate teachings of God's Law. God's Law is therefore ultimately normative for the positive legislation of the state.

In his *Law and Customs of England*, the great 13th-century English jurist Henry de Bracton (c. 1210-1268), who exerted such a vast Christian influence on the entire history of Anglo-Saxon law (the common law), writes:

> The king himself, however, ought not to be under man but under God, and under Law, because the Law makes the king.[1] Therefore, let the king render back to the Law

[1] By the law, Bracton means all divine and human laws: first of all, the eternal law which illuminates natural law, which is merely the physical and moral order given to creation by God, an order that refracts itself in true reason and in the conscience of man. This natural law from God is expressed more or less adequately in the positive law of nations. Its purest expression is found in biblical law. For Bracton, the moral law contained in the Bible is the final standard by which all natural law—and thus all

> what the Law gives to him, namely dominion and power; *for there is no king where will, and not Law, wields dominion.*[2]

Elsewhere, Bracton writes:

> Now let us see what is law; and we should know that law is the common precept of prudent men in council, the coercive prohibition of offenses which are committed intentionally or by ignorance, the impartial bulwark of the common interests. Also God is the author of justice, because justice is in the Creator. And accordingly, rightness and law *(jus et lex)* signify the same thing, and while in the widest sense everything that can be read is called law, strictly it signifies just sanction, enjoining what is fair and decent and forbidding the contrary.[3]

We must thus make it very clear that Christ Himself is the source of all true, just, and good Law. However, only spiritual power, Christ Himself as a divine and incarnate Mediator between God and mankind, acting through His church, can save and transform man. Temporal power therefore must never trespass beyond its own specific and limited domain and usurp the characteristics of religious power. It must never seek to compete with the church of God. For it then becomes a power with a messianic nature, a power with salvific pretensions. It is from such a presumption that the modern state was born and has become a true earthly *Providence* or *welfare state*. For it is to the state that the people of our day turn to find solutions to their problems, whether physical, spiritual, or moral.

Let us immediately add that, in a corollary way, if the church (as was the case with the imperial papacy of the High Middle Ages) attempts to usurp the authority of temporal power, it also becomes an earthly messianic power with totalitarian tendencies, believing itself to be God.

A glaring and quite common aspect of such an attitude is

---

positive law—must be judged. His position on the various aspects of the law is, on the whole, very similar to that of Thomas Aquinas, although it does not appear that he had the opportunity to read the latter's writings.

[2] Henry de Bracton, *De legibus*, III, O.2, fol. 5b, quoted in John C. H. Wu, *Fountain of Justice: A Study in the Natural Law* (Sheed and Ward, New York, 1955), 73.

[3] Henry de Bracton, *De legibus,* fol. 2, quoted in ibid., 75.

that of our contemporaries in the face of the natural disasters that afflict them. Let's take an example. The farmers of the Swiss canton of Vaud, hit hard in 1976 by a lengthy drought, did not turn to God or to the representative of God here on earth (the church), as was so common in the past during times of public calamity. In the churches of the Reformation, solemn fasts of repentance were held while Roman Catholics sought to appease God's righteous anger against our public and private sins by penitential acts such as public processions. For it was then thought—quite rightly and in a very biblical way—that a cause-and-effect relationship existed between national and social calamities and the wrath of a righteous God against a people's sins.

This bygone mentality (erroneously considered anachronistic) led our dechristianized farmers faced with the scourge of a prolonged drought to turn to what was their true god: the welfare state (with its headquarters in the cantonal castle in Lausanne or the Federal Palace of Bern) and to demand subsidies from these authorities. And, for their part, the clergy of our canton did not for a single instant notice that this was a form of idolatry. At no time were they struck by the idea of calling the people under their care to repentance, to a humbling of themselves before the sovereign God so that He might be appeased in His righteous anger against the many infidelities of His people. For these pastors—imbued as the majority of them were with our modern (dualistic and positivistic Kantian) ideology incapable of perceiving a relationship between God and the events of this world, between divine Providence and meteorology—no longer understand that God has acted (and still does today) through the phenomena of nature and the events of history.

Another example of this redemptive presumption of the state is the very existence of our penitentiaries which, as places of punishment, pretend to become places of social rehabilitation.[4] The state not subject to the Law of God becomes a true totalitarian religion after a humanist model, with both messianic and "redemptive" aims. The religious problem of our time lies not only or even primarily on the explicitly confessional level, but above all in the

---

[4] The word *penitentiary* itself testifies to the state's absorption of the church's duties. The place where, in the Middle Ages, the repentant sinner was called to do "penance" has been replaced by a place of incarceration for criminals, a place where the secular state attempts to "rehabilitate" them.

pretensions of the modern state to manage, for their own good, all areas of human existence.

Christian circles that demand a complete separation between church and state—it is obviously difficult for a pastor in the pay of the state to truthfully and boldly exhort the same state from which he receives his livelihood[5]—have not sufficiently realized that this necessary separation must not have the purpose of abandoning the state to its institutional and spiritual autonomy, to what could be called the *freedom of its administrative conscience.* For the conscience of those who hold power in the state cannot claim to be free. The state cannot evade its imperative duty to conform its action to the requirements of God's Law without incurring, by this pretended autonomy, the judgment of God and consequently bringing destruction upon the country over which it exercises power.

Nor can there be any moral "neutrality" of the state. Either the state is a servant of God for good, accordingly punishing the evildoer and encouraging the one who does good according to the criteria of the Law of God, or it establishes itself as its own standard and thus becomes its own god. It then makes itself the servant of evil and of false justice, distributing injustice rather than justice to those placed under its power. The distinction of the church in relation to the state; its institutional independence and its primary union with God (its unity); and, more importantly, its separation from sin (its holiness), the seductions of the world, and the deceptions of the devil battling against the fulness of its doctrine (its catholicity); and its rejection of doctrinal error (its apostolicity), all have the essential purpose of enabling the church to fulfill the exercise of its own spiritual authority. This is so that she might fully exercise her prophetic ministry through the clarity and power of the preaching of the Word of God, both law and gospel, gospel and law, not only to individuals but to all the corporate institutions of society and, above all, to those who exercise their authority over us for good or for ill. It is through such spiritual means that she can work to lead every person and every social institution to repentance and salvation.

In particular, as far as concerns us here, the church's preach-

---

[5] Since the fundamental conflict in the mid-16th century between Pierre Viret and Theodore Beza on the one hand and the Bernese authorities on the other, the Vaud State Church has been largely paralyzed by its almost universal unbiblical submission to the public authorities.

ing of the Law-Word of God must seek to remind public authorities that their power must be exercised in full submission to the principles expressed in the Law of God. It is only through such a submission of the political realm and of jurisprudence to divine law that the preamble to the Swiss Federal Constitution and the founding documents of American jurisprudence—which purport to express themselves "in the name of Almighty God"—can become a reality in the laws as well as in the public life of our country. God must first be served in the church. Yet He must equally enjoy the first place in the state. It is to ensure this dual submission of the church and the state to the divine commands that spiritual and temporal power should be better distinguished in the institutions of our country.

Within Switzerland and other countries, a state church still exists, a national institution under the oversight of the civil authorities. Unfortunately, since the 18th century Enlightenment, these cantonal churches have generally become infected with the rationalist errors of our modern atheistic secularization. The biblical Revivals of the 19th century that occurred in our Protestant cantons largely issued from within these state churches but were systematically rejected by them.

In contrast to this, what are known as "free" or independent evangelical circles are those which are intrinsically independent of the civil government and which thus enjoy a measure of autonomy from the political sphere. As long as they have existed, these free evangelical circles have in fact been separated from the state. But when have these circles preached the Word of God, prayed to God and obeyed God's commands in such a way that the secularization of the state—that is, its independence from God's Law, its practical atheism—was effectively denounced, curbed, or stopped by the covenantal obedience of God's church?

No, these circles' assertion of their strict separation between church and state has too often been a way (no doubt unconscious) of washing their hands of their Christian responsibility to the public authorities.[6] Thus, for lack of the faithful preaching of the full

---

[6] This is where the essential error of Alexandre Vinet and the entire evangelical movement of the 19th century revival in French-speaking Switzerland, which sought above all the "freedom of worship" in relation to the state, lies. For the Christian, the defense of doctrinal truth must take priority over the institutional freedom of the church. On these issues, see Jean-Marc Berthoud, *Des Actes de l'Église.* See also Jean-Marc Berthoud, *L'Histoire Alliancielle de l'Église dans le Monde,* Volume 4, *L'Âge Moderne: De la*

counsel of God, the entire public sphere was surrendered to the evil forces that sought to divert it from its creational purpose: to glorify God in the public life of the secular realm. Their independence from the state, instead of being a means to better engage the battle (since these circles were free from the shackles of institutional submission to the state), became merely a means for these independent churches to utterly abandon the battle of bringing the light of divine Truth to shine within the public sphere. The danger that threatened them, and which they were utterly unaware of, was that of an evangelical pietism that limited Jesus Christ's accomplished work of salvation to the "soul" of the individual and thus to the church. Some of these circles have created an ideological justification for this public resignation in the antinomian theory of *dispensationalism* which relegates any practical application of God's Law to a pre-Christian Jewish past and projects the reality of the kingdom into the distant future of the establishment of an imaginary millennial messianic reign of Israel over the entire earth.[7]

But it is not only free or independent evangelical circles that are calling for a total separation between church and state. For the last two centuries and more, this has been one of the explicit goals of all politically atheist or agnostic circles. The politically antinomian spectrum ranges from the Freemasons and their liberal allies (radicals) to socialists, communists, and today the environmentalists and the gender oriented fanatics. The culmination of this systematic dechristianization of political life is the emergence of a supposedly neutral technocratic state but one which is in reality anti-theistic and antichristian.[8] The logical materialization of this so-called real-

---

*Révolution scientifique aux Révolutons politiques et culturelles: Le réveil, la réponse divine à un monde sans Dieu* (Messages, Lausanne, Lulu.com, 2019); Frédéric de Rougemont, *The Individualists in Church and State*.

[7] See the following books which give the Scriptural foundations for rejecting these farfetched interpretations of the Bible: Curtis I. Crenshaw and Grover E. Gunn, *Dispensationalism, Today, Yesterday, and Tomorrow* (Footstool Publications, Memphis, Tennessee, 1985); John H. Gerstner, *Wrongly Dividing the Word of Truth: A Critique of Dispensationalism* (Wolgemuth and Hyatt, Brentwood, Tennessee, 1991); Philip Mauro, *The Hope of Israel: What is it?* (Reiner Publications, Swengel, Pennsylvania, 1970); *The Gospel of the Kingdom with an Examination of Dispensationalism* (Reiner Publications, Swengel, 1974); Hans K. LaRondelle, *The Israel of God in Prophecy: Principles of Prophetic Interpretation* (Andrews University Press, Berrien Springs, 1983).

[8] The terms *secular* or *secularized* usually used to describe this phenomenon should be systematically replaced with *atheist* or *antichristian*. This is the "godless" phenomenon so aptly denounced by all Christian opponents of the Russian Revolution.

ity was clearly revealed in the project to construct a world (cosmos) from which God and His Law would have been systematically excluded: the most striking expression of this project in the twentieth century was that of an entirely immanent totalitarianism, that of the Nazi and Communist states. With them, the veil of neutrality was torn down and the state openly proclaimed itself atheist, without God and against God. The open persecution of Christians was the mark of this total rejection of the politically normative nature of God's Law.

The hammer and sickle of communism simply replaced the trowel and square of Freemasonry as signs of man's redemptive work. This is the meaning of the Marxist and Nazi slogan *"Arbeit macht frei,"* "Work makes one free," which was inscribed above the entrance gate at Auschwitz and was the pedagogical motivation of the Soviet and Maoist labor camps. This is the doctrine of the salvation of man through man, of the redemptive political transformation of man through the technical works of man. Salvation through works thus moved from the theological sphere (Pelagianism, semi-Pelagianism, Arminianism) to the political, technical, and cultural domain. This is the secular extension of the salvation by works of Pelagian and Arminian circles. These Freemasons and their allies labored to separate the church from the state because it was necessary for them to abolish all public influence of the church, an influence they deemed harmful because it undermined the freedom and autonomy of man who had finally come of age—that is, who had finally become his own god.

What these circles wanted—and what they openly proclaimed despite all the deist pretensions of Freemasonry—was nothing less than to remove the state, the temporal power, from all dependence on God; this biblical God who is no other than the very origin, purpose, and standard of every state. This was attempted in order that the sword of the state might no longer impose respect for God's Law upon men and that they might instead do entirely as they please. The other goal pursued by these circles was the separation of the churches—officially recognized or not—from any kind of normative submission to the Word of God.[9] At present these two goals

---

[9] A heavily-documented study of this destruction of the biblical foundations of an entire Christian denomination is given in Gary North's excellent work, *Crossed Fingers: How the Liberals Captured the Presbyterian Church* (Institute for Christian Economics, Tyler, 1996). A similar study devoted to the destruction of the Roman Catholic Church

have been very widely accomplished, especially in the antichristian and godless West, the victor of Nazi and communist totalitarianism, but vanquished by their atheistic ideologies.[10] Who among Christians would still dare affirm that positive legislation should conform itself to God's Law to please God and promote the general good of all? Or that abortionists, adulterers, and homosexuals should, according to the clear teaching of the Bible, be punished by the sword of the state? Because such an exercise of human justice by the state is, in our modern Sodom, a political impossibility, we must leave such judgments to the discretion of Almighty God.

The purpose of these various antichristian movements has been very widely achieved in my own country of Switzerland. This came about not through a separation of church and state (a separation no longer necessary since both have largely abandoned the normative authority of the Law of God) but by the destruction of the faithful preaching of the Word of God in the state churches and by the evacuation of its content—in favor of an emotionally non-doctrinal religion—in most evangelical circles.[11] With that mission

---

as a force capable of resisting the systematic atheization of modern society by Vatican II remains to be written. See Dietrich von Hildebrand, *La vigne ravagée* (Éditions du Cèdre, Paris, 1974); *Le cheval de Troie dans la cité de Dieu* (Beauchesne, Paris, 1971); Ralph M. Wiltgen, *Le Rhin se jette dans le Tibre* (Dominique Martin Morin, Bouère, 1992).

[10] On the universal atheization of thought, action, and institutions in the West, see Cornelio Fabro, *Introduction à l'athéisme moderne* (Anne Sigier, Sillery, Québec, 1999); Augusto del Noce, *L'irreligion occidentale* (Fac, Paris, 1995); *Il problema dell'ateisomo* (Il Mulino, Bologna, 1990); *The Crisis of Modernity* (McGill-Queens University Press, Montreal, 2014); John Blanchard, *Does God Believe in Atheists?* (Evangelical Press, 2000); Michael J. Buckley, *At the Origins of Modern Atheism* (Yale University Press, 1987); Vincent P. Miceli, *The Gods of Atheism* (Roman Catholic Books, Harrison, New York, 1971). See also the many books by E. Michael Jones.

[11] On the attack on the Bible within the heart of Protestant churches, see Pierre Marcel, *Face à la critique: Jésus et les apôtres: Esquisse d'une logique chrétienne* (Labor et Fides-Kerygma, Genève-Aix-en-Provence, 1986); François Laplanche, *La Bible en France entre mythe et critique XVIe-XIXe siècles* (Albin Michel, 1994); Jean-Marie Paul, *Dieu est mort en Allemagne: Des Lumières à Nietzsche* (Payot, Paris, 1994); Henning Graf Reventlow, *The Authority of the Bible and the Rise of the Modern World* (SCM Press, London, 1984); Hans W. Frei, *The Eclipse of the Biblical Narrative: A Study in Eighteenth and Nineteenth Century Hermeneutics* (Yale University Press, New Haven, 1974). For a description of similar developments within the Roman Catholic Church, see Dominique Tassot's classic work, *La Bible au risque de la science de Galilée au P. Lagrange* (F. X. de Guibert, Paris, 1997). On the role of certain Jewish circles in this war against the Bible, see Rabbi Marvin S. Antelman, *To Eliminate the Opiate: An In-depth Study of Communist and Conspiratorial Group Efforts to Destroy Jews and Judaism* (2004 [1974]).

accomplished, our "secularists" clearly understood that the question of a possible separation of church and state is no longer relevant. The official churches (emptied of the Word of God) only too faithfully serve the designs of the antichristian forces in society.[12] And the inanity of most of the so-called "evangelical" churches which, through their conformity to the surrounding society and culture, have become socially and culturally irrelevant, have made it superfluous for their atheist opponents to even bother dealing with them.[13]

Among the slogans of these antichristians of every stripe—and their ideological followers, including Protestants, Roman Catholics, Evangelicals, and Jews—we find the following expressions:

> *Pluralism:* all truths are good—that is, an absolute truth or unchanging law no longer exists.
> *Tolerance:* tolerance for good and evil; both are on an equal footing—that is, there must no longer be a repression of evil or a praise of good.
> *Freedom:* the "freedom of conscience" has now become the freedom to create one's own definition of good and evil.
> *Fraternity:* all are brothers; no more hierarchical, social, or family distinctions exist, which leads to the atomization and uniformization of society. But, above all, we must abolish the distinction between children of God and children of the world; no more holiness or uncleanness; no more lost or saved. "We are all children of God" read a poster for a Christian Science conference in Lausanne.
> *Equality:* the equality of all "truth claims" of all religions. This is the interchangeable equality of "good" and "evil": pure Taoism.

---

[12] For Switzerland, we can simply take the latest version of the federal family legislation which destroys any legal support for the Christian order of the family—and this without any protest from the churches. As far as the churches are concerned, the examples are innumerable: we can simply take the fact that the *Centre Social Protestant* of Lausanne, in supporting the solution of delayed abortion, merely incites—in the name of Christ—the people of its canton to murder their own children.

[13] See, among many other books for a similar American diagnosis, David F. Wells, *God in the Wasteland* (Eerdmans, Grand Rapids, 1994); *No Place for Truth* (Eerdmans, 1993); *Losing our Virtue* (Eerdmans, 1998).

True Christians must completely dissociate themselves from any even apparent collaboration with these atheistic tendencies and must especially be careful to cleanse their language of this liberal antichristian jargon. *In particular, we should speak of politics in the same way the Bible does.*

Let us add that Scripture teaches us, particularly in chapters thirteen, seventeen, and eighteen of Revelation, that the false church, without God, without the Word of God, without faith or law, will also be supported by a state devoid of the Law of God. We have already seen this occurring for some time. It will continue even more so when the pluralist and syncretistic church draws all its strength from the atheist state, and this under the elegant mantle of a humanitarianism that will deceive the majority of those who are not watchful. The true church of God, institutionally distinct from but in no way opposed to the power of the state, has, among other tasks entrusted to it by God, that of working toward the reestablishment of the functioning of the state in the order intended for it by God. That is, the church labors to see that the exercise of public power conforms to the requirements of the Bible's political mandate as defined by the Law of God.

Some Christians claim that "the absolute equality (as much as is possible) of all religious or philosophical attitudes and of all houses of worship is the surest guarantee of freedom of conscience for everyone."[14] Is this true?

The Christian knows that the only true freedom is conformity to the truth, to the sole good, to God, through faith in Christ and with the assistance of the Holy Spirit. Just as much in the church realm as in the family, school, business, state, and in short in all spheres of life, the only true freedom is that which leads us to conform ourselves, in Christ, to the creation order established and desired by God. This is the truth that sets us free—not the pluralism of lies. Such pluralism can only lead to anarchy, and anarchy will lead to totalitarianism, the seizure of power by the most powerful and vicious political group which will restore a certain "order" to society by imposing—often by the use of the most brutal force—the absolute values of its own choice. This is the fatal alternative that the philosopher Jean Brun indicated in the startling phrase "Dictatorship or putrefaction." Separated from God and deprived of His good

---

[14] *Mémoire concernant la séparation des Églises et de l'État en Suisse* (May 1977), 2.

Law, men are indeed trapped between such a terrifying choice.

But there is another solution for the world. This is what true Christianity offers. For we don't simply assert our own "opinions," equal in value to the "opinions" of someone else. No, we unashamedly and unreservedly affirm that we know the infallible and understandable revelation of the one God, the Law-Word of God, the Bible which gives us the plan of the order the Creator established for His creation and which is the sole basis of all true freedom and all true human happiness. For, since He is the Creator, God alone knows what we His creatures stand in need of. Thus we boldly affirm: *the only guarantee of true freedom for a people is respect—by the state, all constituted bodies of the nation, and by its citizens—for the Law of God.* The adoption of the noxious principles of pluralist tolerance— a tolerance of both good and evil—inevitably leads (because of sin) to the inescapable increase of evil and, in the long run, to the people and the state's absolute intolerance of all that represents the order God has willed for this earth.

Other Christians argue that "freedom of conscience urgently demands the complete neutrality of the state in relation to all churches and sects."[15]

Let us first consider this notion of "neutrality" that is so dear to liberal thought. Such neutrality is simply impossible! No one can serve two masters. The state must act either *for* the application of the Law of God—that is, for God and for the common good—or *against* the application of God's Law, i.e., against the God who gave this Law and for the generalization of evil. This opposition to God and His Law may vary depending on circumstances, even in a government that does not explicitly acknowledge the laws of its Creator. For, though the perfect reign of Christ is hardly for today, yet even the most tyrannical of governments cannot remove all traces of the Law of God from their administration without making it impossible for human society to survive. All respect for the Law of God has not yet entirely disappeared from our societies. If the state is for God's Law, it will affirm, uphold, and enforce the distinction between spiritual and temporal power and will limit its own activities to those delegated to it by God's Law—primarily to the exercise of justice on a domestic level and in its foreign policies. It will indirectly favor the development of Christian churches through its public affirmation

---
[15] Ibid., 2.

of the authority of God's Law. The judicial severity with which it punishes evildoers will greatly facilitate the public's understanding of the need for repentance to approach the thrice-holy God.

In a family where the parents justly and honestly battle against evil, the children will learn to recognize the difference between good and evil. The same is true of the state. Where the magistrate handles criminals with just severity and exonerates the innocent, the people will understand the difference between justice and crime. If the state claims neutrality, this "neutrality" will only encourage all errors and, in the end, by its very pluralism it will make it much more difficult for the people to hear the Truth, even within faithful churches.

Moreover, the famous notion of *freedom of conscience* is dangerous and must be handled with care. If it merely means the Christian's refusal to impose faith upon unbelievers through the violence of the sword or manipulative techniques, there can be little problem with it. Spiritual power, proceeding from God, must remain spiritual. Temporal power, also proceeding from God, must remain temporal. Any mixture of the two powers leads to totalitarian tyranny. But within the notion of *freedom of conscience,* much more is often included.

The Bible teaches us that, like moral neutrality, what we call freedom of conscience simply does not exist. *Since man is created in the image of God, his true conscience is linked to God's Law-Word.* Within all realms of various liberal circles, the notion of a freedom of conscience supposedly autonomous from any duty of submission to the Law of God is merely a war machine used to bind the conscience to lies, error, and evil. This is the freedom of conscience that the serpent so seductively offered Eve. This so-called "freedom" of conscience is nothing more than the possibility given to man by God to freely damn himself. Therefore, mankind can never know such freedom of conscience in the sense that the liberals use this term. The reason is that every man—whether he recognizes it or not makes no difference—can only live within the objective limits fixed for him by his Creator. The wages of this "freedom of conscience" advocated by the liberals is exactly the same as what the Bible grants to sin: eternal, spiritual, intellectual, physical, familial, ecclesiastical, national, artistic, scientific, political, ecological death for man and society.

It goes without saying that the exercise of the power of the sword is limited to public crimes; it cannot proceed beyond that because it has no power over people's thoughts or over their consciences. Only the church has a (limited) authority over consciences, and her influence is only exercised by spiritual means. Nor can she pretend to read the hearts of her members. This area is reserved for God alone. Here, any abuse and mixture of temporal and spiritual powers can only lead to the inquisition of consciences and minds and to the high-tech totalitarian control of bodies.

The final point to note is the religious nature of the modern state. A humanist, humanitarian religion is now everywhere being imposed, more and more effectively, on the whole world by quasi-omnipotent states under the domination of invisible influences. The church of this humanist religion is none other than a culture issuing from the secular schools and universities—that is, a type of instruction devoid of God, His Law, and the order of His creation. This culture is imposed by a messianic compulsory educational system (both private and public) which has become an instrument of spiritual and social transformation. This the Bible calls the second beast, the prostitute or the false prophet (Rev. 13 and 17). The godless state takes the children of parents of all religious or philosophical convictions and seeks to make of them creatures in its own image. This seems to me to be the true spiritual battle of our time. Humanism, the ideology of the godless state which has largely divorced itself from the Law of God and God's created order, has in truth become a religion, a truly mandatory religion. To understand its true power, one must only attempt to evade its abusive demands.

Isn't it unjust, and a crying injustice, to compel all (or almost all) children to attend a secular school in which all subjects of study are taught as if the living God simply didn't exist? And if we refuse this secular teaching and choose to send our children to "religious" schools, we must (besides paying the fees for these private schools) pay taxes for a service in which our children don't even participate! It is at this crucial point that we must begin the battle: first in favor of the multiplication of Christian homeschooling, then the establishment of schools in which the teaching given would truly conform to the Law of God; and secondly to work that the atheist state might begin to abandon its totalitarian religious pretensions. This implies a resolute separation of the state's activity from its present religious functions, such as that of education itself, which it has absolutely no business being involved in. But we Christians, obsessed as we so often are with the world's thinking, stubbornly refuse to remove our children from the midst of this perverse generation (Acts 2:40). In our unconsciousness, we often fail to even perceive the problem and, without a twinge of conscience, we throw our children not to the beasts (as was done in Roman times) but to the ruthless Beast, this state devoid of God or Law or a created order which Scripture speaks of:

> Thus he said, The fourth beast shall be the fourth kingdom upon earth, which shall be diverse from all kingdoms, and shall devour the whole earth, and shall tread it down, and break it in pieces. (Dan. 7:23)

This verse must be read in connection with what Paul wrote to the Thessalonians:

> Let no man deceive you by any means: for that day shall not come, except there come a falling away first, and that man of sin[16] be revealed, the son of perdition; who opposeth and exalteth himself above all that is called God, or that is worshipped; so that he as God sitteth in the temple of God, shewing himself that he is God. (2 Thess. 2:3-4)

These verses must also be read in connection with the following:

> And they worshipped the dragon which gave power unto the beast: and they worshipped the beast, saying, Who is like unto the beast? who is able to make war with him? (Rev. 13:4)

The humanist socialist state—devoid of God's Law—in which we find ourselves is a political beast, a true Leviathan that has almost completely engulfed us. This political Leviathan is nothing but this beast of which Revelation speaks, and the religion of this state is the humanist atheist culture, the worship of Man. It is here and nowhere else that the Christian battle of our time lies. With the Roman Empire, the early church was faced with a similar struggle.

---

[16] Or "man of lawlessness," that is, lawless humanism incarnate.

This empire was defeated by the faith and obedience of Christians. Faced with the totalitarian papal Rome of the sixteenth century, the Reformers and faithful Christians had to engage in a similar battle. They also won great victories against this new Leviathan, the apocalyptic Beast of their time. But the Christians relaxed, and the victory was relinquished to godless humanism.

Due to numerous factors which include the worldwide generalization of an obligatory state (or state subsidized) secular educational system, a very widespread mental framework, exclusive of any kind of divine transcendence or immanence, has been put into place. This has been accompanied by the apparently irresistible growth of a "technological cocoon" which largely protects the majority of people in our developed nations from direct contact with the hard and often brutal realities of life. This leads to the development of a mentality (that is, a culture and manner of thinking) which finds it difficult to acknowledge any kind of truth excluded by a generally accepted intellectual consensus deprived of all absolutes.[17]

With the rise of absolutism and its culmination in the revolutionary state, faithful Christians face new battles. Faced with the forthcoming alliance of universal Judeo-Christian apostasy (in which the second syncretistic Rome will no doubt play a crucial role) and ecological, social democratic, pantheistic globalism, we must now reignite the torch of the faith in the truth of the ancient martyrs. We must begin again this battle of all ages so that even today the kingdom of God might come upon earth as in heaven. May God once again strengthen His church. *Amen. Come, Lord Jesus!*

---

[17] See the following very suggestive cultural, sociological, and psychological studies describing these mental changes: David Riesman, Nathan Glazer, and Reuel Denney, *The Lonely Crowd: A Study of the Changing American Character* (Yale University Press, 1950); *Individualism Reconsidered* (The Free Press, 1954); J. H. van den Berg, *The Changing Nature of Man: Introduction to a Historical Psychology* (Dell Publishing Co., New York, 1961); Jacques Barzun, *The Culture We Deserve* (Wesleyan University Press, Middletown, 1989); Pitirim A. Sorokin, *The Crisis of our Age* (Oneworld, Oxford, 1992 [1941]); *The American Sex Revolution* (Peter Sargent, Boston, 1956); Harold O. J. Brown, *The Sensate Culture: Western Civilization Between Chaos and Transformation* (Word Publishing, Dallas, 1996); Henry R. Van Til, *The Calvinist Concept of Culture* (Presbyterian and Reformed, Philadelphia, 1972); Joseph Siri, "La Culture," chapter VII of Jean-Marc Berthoud, *L'Histoire alliancielle de l'Église dans le Monde*, volume V.

## SIXTEEN

# Conclusion

We find ourselves in a very special historical and spiritual situation, and our salvation requires us to recognize it. We must not confuse the righteous power of God exercised by fallible men to whom He has delegated it with the unlimited power of the "man of sin" manifested through an anonymous and largely amoral bureaucratic and technocratic state. Everywhere we look we witness the deification of the humanitarian state—now become an earthly Providence—from whence comes our help and which assumes an ever more and more messianic function in its charitable, medical, and redemptive aspects. It is from this state that mankind hopes to receive the solutions to all its problems, yet these solutions are no more than impotent palliatives because they place themselves outside the covenantal framework established by the Law of God, outside of the respect of these intermediate bodies that the Creator has established between the individual and the state. This bureaucratic, anonymous, impersonal, and irresponsible power imposed either by force or by cunning is undermining and destroying the order established by God and has been universally accepted out of fear, helplessness, laziness, unconcern, and ignorance. Its unrelenting growth is marked by the constant expansion of the centralizing bureaucratic apparatus of the state. It is a power that is the fruit of ungodliness, injustice, countless evil deeds, and the lies of men who have forgotten their obligations to God and their neighbor. This is what Scripture metaphorically calls "the power of the beast." We must not confuse the human fallible power given by God with this beastly power, for we would then be in danger of attributing to God what comes from Satan. Woe to us if we so confuse those things which must be absolutely distinguished.

> Woe unto them that call evil good, and good evil; that put

> darkness for light, and light for darkness; that put bitter for sweet, and sweet for bitter! Woe unto them that are wise in their own eyes, and prudent in their own sight! (Isa. 5:20-21)

Our modern world has given way to the temptation of the prince of Tyre evoked by the prophet Ezekiel:

> Son of man, say unto the prince of Tyrus, Thus saith the Lord GOD; Because thine heart is lifted up, and thou hast said, I am a God, I sit in the seat of God, in the midst of the seas; yet thou art a man, and not God, though thou set thine heart as the heart of God: behold, thou art wiser than Daniel; there is no secret that they can hide from thee: with thy wisdom and with thine understanding thou hast gotten thee riches, and hast gotten gold and silver into thy treasures: by thy great wisdom and by thy traffick hast thou increased thy riches, and thine heart is lifted up because of thy riches: . . . Wilt thou yet say before him that slayeth thee, I am God? but thou shalt be a man, and no God, in the hand of him that slayeth thee. Thou shalt die the deaths of the uncircumcised by the hand of strangers: for I have spoken it, saith the Lord GOD. (Eze. 28:2-10)

We must confess with Georges Bernanos:

> For me, I know which god I deny. It is precisely the monstrous judicial instrument of oppression and destruction called the modern State, the absolute State—the trust of trusts and the technocrat of technocrats—from whom the world hopes to receive what the Jews awaited from their Messiah when they nailed Jesus to the cross, that is, not a redemption by God made man, but by Man made god.[1]

Above all, in this time of terrible spiritual dangers, we must not take sides with evil, with the beast, with the ungodly, with the absolute state. We must utterly refuse to take sides with the "inevitable progress" of a science which has broken free from the created or-

---

[1] Georges Bernanos, *Français si vous saviez* (Gallimard, Paris, 1961), 159.

der or with the pretended "progressive development" of a resolutely godless society. We must not take the mark of the beast either on our hand (through our work to build a society whose sole purpose is the satisfaction of the glory of *Man* who proclaims himself to be god; 2 Thess. 2:4) or on our forehead (by abandoning the very thinking of God in all areas of human life and action). We must repudiate this rejection of the Law of God, of the gospel of the kingdom. We must refuse to attach ourselves to all philosophies liberated from divine thought, to all sciences of nature and of man which are resolutely independent of the created order. For they draw their thoughts from themselves and deny the reality created by God and the Creator God Himself, proceeding with the aim of constructing a world-cosmos without God and opposed to God and thus further leading men astray into the darkness of lies, error, and injustice.

Let us not, through our deeds and thoughts, collaborate in the building of the earthly kingdom of the man of sin (the *anomos*, the one "without law"), a kingdom established on technology and science, finance and culture, all entirely liberated from the constraints of the natural order as established by divine law. In short, let us refuse to be seduced by an utterly humanistic messianism leading us all directly to the godless religion of the worship of Man who thinks he is God.

The Holy Scriptures speak to us of the beastly state which no longer exercises an authority proceeding from God but instead the power of the prince of this world acting through lawless and faithless men—the tares of the parable, a symbol that represents the children of the evil one—to reverse the order of time as established by God as well as the Law of God itself (Dan. 7:25). And of this evil power of a state tempted to be seduced by the powers of evil, we are told not to take the number—let alone the mark—on our hand or forehead. The hand here represents work or labor, and the forehead represents the realm of thought. The number of the beast, 666, the great Babylon, is the kingdom of man devoid of God.

And, if we live today under this beastly power, what must we do to remain truly faithful to God? What is our part to be played in this life of faithful perseverance and believing in obedience to God? We know what young Daniel and his three friends had to do to remain pure before their God when they were placed in the palace of Nebuchadnezzar, the idolatrous and ungodly king of Babylon. They refused to eat the unclean food offered to them. So what are the culinary dishes (cultural trends) that we must *voluntarily* deprive ourselves of so that we might not participate in the power of darkness rising from the abyss and becoming daily more and more tangible around us? We have seen too many so-called Christians, by compromise with the banality of a so-called "Christianity" fashioned after the culture of the day, enter with guilty disregard and ignorance upon the wide and easy path of apostasy not to ask ourselves such a question with the utmost concern. Scripture warns us: when the hour of darkness comes, is it still possible to work? Christ Himself offered us this warning:

> I must work the works of him that sent me, while it is day: the night cometh, when no man can work. As long as I am in the world, I am the light of the world. (John 9:4-5)

Others have added their own solemn warning:

> When error is once embodied in judicial formulas and administrative practices, it penetrates minds to depths from which it becomes almost impossible to remove it. ... It is then necessary to completely ignore the real conditions of humanity in order not to see how the vice or only the shortcoming of the institutions affects all classes of society and weighs on even the firmest and most independent minds.[2]

> By dint of seeing everything, we end up supporting everything; and by dint of supporting everything, we end up admitting everything.[3]

> If the state is evil, if it is flawed in its doctrines, it ends up stifling the cries of conscience.[4]

In the face of such power, the Christian's task is not to enter into the game of forces that, through interposed parties, compete for the domination of this world of darkness, a world made of a political

---
[2] Cardinal Edward Pie.
[3] Augustine.
[4] Albert de Mun. These three quotations come from the book by Jean Marie Vaissière, *Fondements de la cité* (Cercles canadiens de formation civique, Québec, 1963), 135.

and technocratic sphere increasingly deprived of the light of God. The Christian has a very special task. The Bible shows us that Satan seeks at all times to divert the order that God has established from its purpose—to bring about law and justice—and redirect it away from its intended aim in order to establish the concentration camp regime of the manipulative totalitarian state reigning over people who have been skillfully stripped of every means of material, psychological, moral, or spiritual resistance. The Bible teaches us that this has always been the focus of that battle, still being waged today, by the archangel Michael and the heavenly hosts under his command against Satan and his demonic hordes. Today, we see many signs that allow us to discern that we are reaching one of the highest historical points of this spiritual struggle whose religious, geopolitical, and cosmic significance exceeds anything we can think or imagine. In a struggle whose magnitude could crush us, our firm hope is that today, just like yesterday and tomorrow, God—by the present victory of His saints—will clearly manifest the complete triumph accomplished by Jesus Christ at the cross. We are now in the time of hope, of waiting for this final event in which our Lord will, by His final advent, take *His sovereign power* in hand, an action through which He will fully enter His reign (Rev. 11:17).

But, while awaiting that blessed hour, it is up to the body of Christ, the faithful church, to take its part on earth in this heavenly battle. Our humble obedience in the little daily things God asks of us certainly plays a much more important role in this combat than we imagine. For too often we judge what is happening and what is truly important by the shifting standards of this fallen world and not according to the eternal criteria of the Spirit—that is, according to what Holy Scripture teaches. In this dreadful and wonderful battle, the Christian must fight through the Spirit, offering requests, prayers, entreaties, and thanksgiving to God, speaking the truth to authorities, interceding for all men, for kings and all who exercise power, in order that an island of freedom, peace, and justice may be granted them (1 Tim. 2:1-3).

In this purpose, the church of God also has a duty to remind those in authority of their responsibilities, in order that they might use the power God has entrusted to them according to truth and justice—that is, according to the standards of the Law of God. But the church must not, out of unbelief or ambition, seek to substitute itself for temporal power, believing that it can better exercise it than those to whom God has delegated it. For, by doing so, she would claim, now and in an illusory way, to enter into the fulness of the dominion of the kingdom of God.[5] This usurpation by the church of the power that only belongs to Jesus Christ at His return is nothing more than the beginning of the modern revolutionary movement—a truly earthly messianism—the kingdom of God reduced to purely immanent political, social, secular, and cultural action.[6]

It would here be very useful to study the three temptations of Christ in the desert, which can also be understood as the major temptations of His body, the church:

1. The *social* temptation: stones turned into bread
2. The *political* temptation: to rule all the kingdoms of the earth *now* through the power of Satan
3. The *spiritualist* temptation: to replace humble obedience to the commandments of God—accomplished with the help of the various graces of the Holy Spirit—with the search for supernatural signs from de-

---

[5] This was the temptation to which the imperial papacy of the High Middle Ages succumbed.

[6] The vision of the kingdom of God defended by the World Council of Churches is nothing more than a syncretistic political, social, and cultural messianism quite unrelated to the biblical teaching of the kingdom of God. This religious and political messianism is very well suited to all messianisms and all pagan religions. On these issues see, among many other works: Walter Ullmann, *The Growth of Papal Government in the Middle Ages* (Methuen, London, 1955); Georges de Lagarde, *La naissance de l'esprit laïque au déclin du Moyen-Age,* five volumes (Nauwelaerts, Louvain, 1956-1963). See also the works by Francis Oakley, *Omnipotence, Covenant and Order: An Excursion in the History of Ideas from Abelard to Leibniz* (Cornell University Press, Ithaca, 1984) and *Politics and Eternity: Studies in the History of Medieval and Early-Modern Political Thought* (Brill, Leiden, 1999).

The notions of "papal power" (Ullmann), the "secular spirit" (of Lagarde), and "omnipotence" (Oakley) are, on closer inspection, closely linked to each other. It is the claim of omnipotence set forth by the papal government of the Roman Church (the latter taking the place of God's sovereignty) which has, by reaction and imitation, become the engine of the modern secular spirit which excludes all transcendence from human affairs. Machiavelli and Hobbes, one might say, are disciples of Gregory VII, Innocent III, and Boniface VIII. On the other hand, it was against such omnipotence that Thomas Aquinas, Henry de Bracton, Pierre de Seyssel, Martin Bucer, Pierre Viret, John Calvin, and Theodore Beza fought—followed later by Edmund Burke, Johann Georg Hamann, Friedrich Julius Stahl, Vladimir Guettée, Donoso Cortes, Groen van Prinsterer, Georges Bernanos, R. J. Rushdoony, Pierre Courthial, and Aleksandr Solzhenitsyn.

monic spirits that arouse so-called apparitions and effortlessly counterfeit the gifts of the Holy Spirit

Here we can discern the great temptation to which the Roman Catholic Church succumbed. For she largely forgot the true nature of her call to be the salt of the earth, the light of the world, the beginnings of the kingdom of God and the herald of Jesus Christ in this world. Thus, as we see in the history of the medieval church, the imperial ambitions of the Church of Rome prevailed over its evangelical calling and it sought, wherever it could, to dominate over temporal power and to hold this power in political subordination. It is by following the example of the Roman Church that the English, French, and Spanish monarchs also came to claim the absolute rights of a state constituted as its own end outside the standards set by God for the just exercise of its power.

By usurping temporal power, the Roman Church abandoned the covenant of God and ceased to be that salt of the earth whose flavor was to curtail the increasing corrupt action of the evil one over peoples and nations (Lev. 2:12-13). Thus, through the misplaced and unbelieving ambition of the one who still claimed to hold the keys of the kingdom of God, the leaven of disobedience to God had free rein to permeate the entire dough of the Christian nations of its time. By the Roman Church's abdication of its spiritual responsibilities, the one (the devil) who seeks the complete destruction of God's creation watched as the obstacle—a faithful church and state, each within its own domain—that had until then prevented the fulfillment of his destructive action, utterly disappeared (2 Thess. 2:6).[7]

Let us again recall that the power of the church is *spiritual,* and the Word she proclaims by the Holy Spirit is *normative* for all areas of human life and existence. This includes the exercise of temporal power, for the church has received from God the task of teaching what the standard of God's Word tells us concerning all the orders of creation. The *material power* of the church—that is, its power of self-discipline—can only be exercised over its own members. If the church usurps the exercise of temporal power by commanding

---

[7] For a fundamental critique of the institution of the papacy, see Vladimir Guettée, *De la papauté* (L'Âge d'Homme, Lausanne, 1990). These historical questions have been carefully studied and explained in the five volumes of Jean-Marc Berthoud, *L'Histoire alliancielle de l'Église dans le monde [The Covenantal History of the Church in the World]* (Messages, Lausanne, Lulu.com, 2018-2020).

the state as master (like the imperial papacy did), it loses its legitimacy and transforms itself into a church-state—the junction of the two beasts of Revelation thirteen—invested with totalitarian ambitions. One of the first signs of such a deviation in the church is the persecution of believers, whom she calls "heretics," by the temporal power which has become the inquisitorial servant of the church, an instrument of pure injustice in the hands of the ecclesiastical harlot. This is what happened during the reign of Pope Innocent III, who decreed that all lay people who gathered to read the Bible in their own homes were worthy of death. This was the "heresy" of the Vaudois of Piedmont who were targeted at the same time.

In its erroneous messianic zeal, such a totalitarian and monist church-state—here the medieval church with imperial pretensions—falsely imagined that the final reign of God was intended for that particular age.[8] This led the church to illegitimately arrogate, from that moment forward, the exercise of Christ's power to judge the nations. To do this, the Roman Church invented the heresy according to which the church became the mere extension of the full Person of Jesus Christ, and the pope, the bishop of Rome, usurping the authority of the local churches, came to pretend to be the very vicar of Christ Himself on earth.[9] This is the very political earthly messianism to which the apostate Jews aspired in the time of Jesus Christ. Just as the Sanhedrin of the Jews crucified the Messiah and killed His disciples, so the Roman Church (which was equally apostate) believed it was honoring God by killing the faithful Christians who opposed its illegitimate and abusive claims.

In the present age, the faithful church constitutes the firstfruits of the kingdom of God. The fulness of this kingdom will not be revealed until later, when the King of Glory, our Lord and Savior Jesus Christ, assumes all power and enters into His full reign. On this glorious day, all knees will bow before Him.

The Reformers restored the Word of God to its central and rightful place in the church. But over the centuries these churches

---

[8] H. X. Arquillière, *L'augustinisme politique: Essai sur la formation des théories politiques au Moyen-Age* (Vrin, Paris, 1972 [1934]).

[9] This is an attack against the distinction defined in AD 451 at Chalcedon concerning the two natures of Jesus Christ united, without confusion or separation, into a single divine Person. The church, by "extending Christ," forgot the distinction between the human and divine natures of the Son of God made man in order to furnish itself with some of the attributes of divinity.

abandoned the Reformation doctrine of a sovereign, infallible, and authoritative Scripture. To defend themselves against the attacks of the Roman Church, the Reformers were led to depend on political states which had embraced Protestantism. Unfortunately, all too often the result was Erastianism, the almost complete dependence of the Protestant churches on the state. It was (among other causes) from this situation that a pietistic spiritualism was born that rendered faith essentially personal. Through this, Protestantism came to deliver society and culture, politics, labor, thought, and finally the soul and body of man, into the hands of apostate individuals whose thought and action had become perfectly autonomous from the demands of God's Law. The state itself was cut off from the source of its authority—that is, from God. It increasingly concentrated all power to itself, asserting itself to be the original source of its authority and its own purpose, being accountable to no one and under no obligation to submit to divine Law.

These Protestant churches, illegitimate heirs of the Reformation, have in their apostasy come so far as to no longer even preach salvation. To an exceptionally large extent, they have now abandoned their own calling: to preach the good news of the kingdom of God and thus to bring all nations to submit to the universally normative teachings of Jesus Christ. And, having put their trust in the state, now fully autonomous of God—or, to express this with apocalyptic symbolism: having sat down atop the beast (Rev. 17:3)—these Protestant churches (despite some protests to the contrary) have ceased to rely on the Word of God. Relying instead on secular states, liberal capitalism, modern mathematical science and the resulting technocracy, all of which were strongly encouraged by this now-apostate Protestantism, these now unbelieving churches have dramatically accelerated the hypertrophy of state power begun in the High Middle Ages under the impetus of the Roman papacy. Through their heterodox teaching, these churches subsequently came to the point of justifying the total secularization of society, thus removing it from the universal authority that the Law of God must exercise over it. Since Vatican II with its full adoption of the norms of the secular modern world, the Roman Catholic Church has also embarked on a similar path. One could almost say that these churches have now managed to conquer the whole of creation, not for God as they should have done, but rather for his enemy, Satan. The ecumenical and syncretistic church that is developing before our eyes, a true spiritual harlot, is a social, political, pluralist, and charismatic church which has voluntarily deprived itself of the enlightenment of the Word of God. She has thus wholly submitted to the tempter and his evil vision of reality.[10]

The particular temptation of Byzantine or Russian Orthodoxy has too often been that of the submission, docility, and servility of the church in the face of the temporal power of the emperor, tsar, or political party. In these Orthodox lands, civil power to a large extent often united temporal and spiritual power in a single person, the tsar, the true god-king. Thus, the tsar's function was heir to the divine monarchies of the Eastern empires of antiquity. Since Peter the Great, this temptation has been reinforced by the introduction in Russia of administrative methods and techniques developed by the West. This trend was simply repeated, with a degree of virulence never previously seen, in the totalitarian dictatorship of Soviet communism. *Freedom can only exist where the clear distinction between temporal and spiritual power is recognized.* The recent freeing of the Russian nation from the bonds of Soviet totalitarianism has given this nation the strength to resist, to some degree, the totalitarian tendencies of the West we have been analyzing. It seems obvious that in the West, unless there is an awakening (most unexpected considering the present condition of Western Christianity), we are living in the twilight of our ancient freedoms in the ever-closer conjunction of a humanist religion, an almost compulsory atheist school, and a deified state.

Thus, on all sides we see the terrible words of the apostate church, the great prostitute, confirmed:

> With [her] the kings of the earth have committed fornication, and the inhabitants of the earth have been made drunk with the wine of her fornication. (Rev. 17:2)

> And upon her forehead was a name written, MYSTERY, BABYLON THE GREAT, THE MOTHER OF HARLOTS AND ABOMINATIONS OF THE EARTH. And I saw the woman drunken with the blood of the saints,

---

[10] The final stage of the church's subjugation to the modern world, without God and against God, was Benedict XVI's encyclical letter, *Caritas in Veritate: On integral human development in charity and truth* (the Vatican, 2009).

> and with the blood of the martyrs of Jesus: and when I saw her, I wondered with great admiration. (Rev. 17:5-6)
>
> I saw a woman sit upon a scarlet coloured beast, full of names of blasphemy, having seven heads and ten horns. (Rev. 17:3)
>
> [She] is become the habitation of devils, and the hold of every foul spirit, and a cage of every unclean and hateful bird. For all nations have drunk of the wine of the wrath of her fornication, and the kings of the earth have committed fornication with her, and the merchants of the earth are waxed rich through the abundance of her delicacies. (Rev. 18:2-3)

This is how God speaks of this unfaithful church, a church that relies on the unholy power of a state both without God and against God which, therefore, merely consolidates the power of evil within the social body. But with what rejoicing is the downfall of both announced in heaven! "Rejoice over her, thou heaven, and ye holy apostles and prophets; for God hath avenged you on her" (Rev. 18:20).

What we can be certain of—so immense is Christ's victory at the cross—is the fact that, if we resist these temptations to which the unfaithful church has succumbed, and if we through the sovereign power of Christ devote ourselves to the humble and hidden battle that we have just set forth, submitting to the order God has established for the life and joy of His creatures on this earth, the very gates of hell itself will not prevail against the victorious assaults of the church of Jesus Christ. And then we will see the satanic power of injustice within the total state yield to the righteous, just, and merciful power exercised by men placed in authority on earth by God Himself.

APPENDIX

# John MacArthur: Christ, not Caesar, is Head of the Church

*The Biblical Response of John MacArthur and Grace Community Church*

*The following text appeared in an article written in* La Lumière du monde *on July 31, 2020.*[1]

Grace Community Church, led by well-known church teacher Pastor John MacArthur, announced this week that it will not comply with California Governor Gavin Newsom's order to stop indoor church services, declaring that "Christ, not Caesar, is Head of the Church."

The church's statement follows the governor's recent announcement that all indoor religious gatherings, in churches or in homes, as well as all restaurants, bars, gyms, hair salons, and barbershops in at least thirty-two counties must cease operations.

On Friday, July 24, 2020, MacArthur said in a church blog post that his church would continue to worship in person.

This statement is remarkable in every way, because:

First of all, it is based directly on the Scriptures, whose authority alone is unquestionably affirmed, above the laws of the state. This clear and firm position is in itself extremely courageous and contrasts strongly with the current attitude of the churches which, in their public debates, content themselves with arguments based on natural law, reason, science, or "the law of the land" out of fear of not being "heard" or of being called "fundamentalist."

Secondly, the writers of this declaration uncompromisingly affirm that the true head of the church is Christ and not the state,

---

[1] "Le Christ, et non César, est le chef de l'Église," *La Lumière du monde,* July 31, 2020, https://lumieremonde.wordpress.com/2020/07/31/le-christ-et-non-cesar-est-le-chef-de-leglise/. Reprinted with permission.

the modern Caesar. In this, they assert their unwavering loyalty and allegiance to Christ, the only *kurios* and the only Lord. The early church was confronted with both the synagogue and the imperial power of Rome, and such an exclusive allegiance to Jesus Christ was seen as a challenge, a political threat, a disturbance of the public order. Christians refused to submit to a Caesar who elevated himself above the King of kings.

Today, the confrontation between the church and an authoritarian Caesar is the same as it was for the early church: the modern secular state seeks to govern the content of worship, to redefine good and evil, to change religion and to usurp the place which belongs to God alone by declaring that no religion can rise above the laws of the Republic. To assert today that Christ alone is Lord involves a refusal to bow the knee to cultural secularism. In France, such a position is unthinkable. It would amount to a crime of high treason.

## Christ, not Caesar, is Head of the Church: A Biblical Case for the Church's Duty to Remain Open[2]

Christ is Lord of all. He is the one true head of the church (Eph. 1:22; 5:23; Col. 1:18). He is also King of kings—sovereign over every earthly authority (1 Tim. 6:15; Rev. 17:14; 19:16). Grace Community Church has always stood immovably on those biblical principles. As His people, we are subject to His will and commands as revealed in Scripture. Therefore we cannot and will not acquiesce to a government-imposed moratorium on our weekly congregational worship or other regular corporate gatherings. Compliance would be disobedience to our Lord's clear commands.

Some will think such a firm statement is inexorably in conflict with the command to be subject to governing authorities laid out in Romans 13 and 1 Peter 2. Scripture does mandate careful, conscientious obedience to all governing authority, including kings, governors, employers, and their agents (in Peter's words, "not only to those who are good and gentle, but also to those who are unreasonable" [1 Pet. 2:18]). Insofar as government authorities do not attempt to assert ecclesiastical authority or issue orders that forbid our obedience to God's law, their authority is to be obeyed whether

---

[2] Reprinted with permission. Accessed August 1, 2020, https://www.gracechurch.org/news/posts/1988.

we agree with their rulings or not. In other words, Romans 13 and 1 Peter 2 still bind the consciences of individual Christians. We are to obey our civil authorities as powers that God Himself has ordained.

However, while civil government is invested with divine authority to rule the state, neither of those texts (nor any other) grants civic rulers jurisdiction over the church. God has established three institutions within human society: the family, the state, and the church. Each institution has a sphere of authority with jurisdictional limits that must be respected. A father's authority is limited to his own family. Church leaders' authority (which is delegated to them by Christ) is limited to church matters. And government is specifically tasked with the oversight and protection of civic peace and well-being within the boundaries of a nation or community. *God has not granted civic rulers authority over the doctrine, practice, or polity of the church.* The biblical framework limits the authority of each institution to its specific jurisdiction. The church does not have the right to meddle in the affairs of individual families and ignore parental authority. Parents do not have authority to manage civil matters while circumventing government officials. And similarly, government officials have no right to interfere in ecclesiastical matters in a way that undermines or disregards the God-given authority of pastors and elders.

When any one of the three institutions exceeds the bounds of its jurisdiction it is the duty of the other institutions to curtail that overreach. Therefore, when any government official issues orders regulating worship (such as bans on singing, caps on attendance, or prohibitions against gatherings and services), he steps outside the legitimate bounds of his God-ordained authority as a civic official and arrogates to himself authority that God expressly grants only to the Lord Jesus Christ as sovereign over His Kingdom, which is the church. His rule is mediated to local churches through those pastors and elders who teach His Word (Matt. 16:18–19; 2 Tim. 3:16–4:2).

Therefore, in response to the recent state order requiring churches in California to limit or suspend all meetings indefinitely, we, the pastors and elders of Grace Community Church, respectfully inform our civic leaders that they have exceeded their legitimate jurisdiction, and faithfulness to Christ prohibits us from observing the restrictions they want to impose on our corporate worship services.

Said another way, it has never been the prerogative of civil government to order, modify, forbid, or mandate worship. When, how, and how often the church worships is not subject to Caesar. Caesar himself is subject to God. Jesus affirmed that principle when He told Pilate, "You would have no authority over Me, unless it had been given you from above" (John 19:11). And because Christ is head of the church, ecclesiastical matters pertain to His Kingdom, not Caesar's. Jesus drew a stark distinction between those two kingdoms when He said, "Render to Caesar the things that are Caesar's, and to God the things that are God's" (Mark 12:17). Our Lord Himself always rendered to Caesar what was Caesar's, but He never offered to Caesar what belongs solely to God.

As pastors and elders, we cannot hand over to earthly authorities any privilege or power that belongs solely to Christ as head of His church. Pastors and elders are the ones to whom Christ has given the duty and the right to exercise His spiritual authority in the church (1 Pet. 5:1-4; Heb. 13:7, 17)—and Scripture *alone* defines how and whom they are to serve (1 Cor. 4:1-4). They have no duty to follow orders from a civil government attempting to regulate the worship or governance of the church. In fact, pastors who cede their Christ-delegated authority in the church to a civil ruler have abdicated their responsibility before their Lord and violated the God-ordained spheres of authority as much as the secular official who illegitimately imposes his authority upon the church. Our church's doctrinal statement has included this paragraph for more than 40 years:

> We teach the autonomy of the local church, free from any external authority or control, with the right of self-government and freedom from the interference of any hierarchy of individuals or organizations (Tit. 1:5). We teach that it is scriptural for true churches to cooperate with each other for the presentation and propagation of the faith. Each local church, however, through its elders and their interpretation and application of Scripture, should be the sole judge of the measure and method of its cooperation. The elders should determine all other matters of membership, policy, discipline, benevolence, and government as well (Acts 15:19-31; 20:28; 1 Cor. 5:4-7, 13; 1 Pet. 5:1-4).

In short, as the church, we do not need the state's permission to serve and worship our Lord as He has commanded. The church is Christ's precious bride (2 Cor. 11:2; Eph. 5:23–27). She belongs to Him alone. She exists by His will and serves under His authority. He will tolerate no assault on her purity and no infringement of His headship over her. All of that was established when Jesus said, "I will build My church; and the gates of Hades will not overpower it" (Matt. 16:18).

Christ's own authority is "far above all rule and authority and power and dominion, and every name that is named, not only in this age but also in the one to come. And [God the Father has] put all things in subjection under [Christ's] feet, and gave Him as head over all things to the church, which is His body, the fullness of Him who fills all in all" (Eph. 1:21–23).

Accordingly, the honor that we rightly owe our earthly governors and magistrates (Rom. 13:7) does not include compliance when such officials attempt to subvert sound doctrine, corrupt biblical morality, exercise ecclesiastical authority, or supplant Christ as head of the church in any other way.

The biblical order is clear: Christ is Lord over Caesar, not vice versa. Christ, not Caesar, is head of the church. Conversely, the church does not in any sense rule the state. Again, these are distinct kingdoms, and Christ is sovereign over both. Neither church nor state has any higher authority than that of Christ Himself, who declared, "All authority has been given to Me in heaven and on earth" (Matt. 28:18).

Notice that we are not making a constitutional argument, even though the First Amendment of the United States Constitution expressly affirms this principle in its opening words: "Congress shall make no law respecting an establishment of religion, or prohibiting the free exercise thereof." The right we are appealing to was not *created* by the Constitution. It is one of those unalienable rights granted solely by God, who ordained human government and establishes both the extent and the limitations of the state's authority (Rom. 13:1–7). Our argument therefore is purposely not grounded in the First Amendment; it is based on the same biblical principles that the Amendment itself is founded upon. The exercise of true religion is a divine duty given to men and women created in God's image (Gen. 1:26–27; Acts 4:18–20; 5:29; cf. Matt. 22:16–22). In other words, freedom of worship is a command of God, not a privilege granted by the state.

An additional point needs to be made in this context. Christ is *always* faithful and true (Rev. 19:11). Human governments are not so trustworthy. Scripture says, "the whole world lies in the power of the evil one" (1 John 5:19). That refers, of course, to Satan. John 12:31 and 16:11 call him "the ruler of this world," meaning he wields power and influence through this world's political systems (cf. Luke 4:6; Eph. 2:2; 6:12). Jesus said of him, "he is a liar and the father of lies" (John 8:44). History is full of painful reminders that government power is easily and frequently abused for evil purposes. Politicians may manipulate statistics and the media can cover up or camouflage inconvenient truths. So a discerning church cannot passively or automatically comply if the government orders a shutdown of congregational meetings—even if the reason given is a concern for public health and safety.

The church by definition is an *assembly*. That is the literal meaning of the Greek word for "church"—*ekklesia*—the assembly of the called-out ones. A non-assembling assembly is a contradiction in terms. Christians are therefore commanded not to forsake the practice of meeting together (Heb. 10:25)—and no earthly state has a right to restrict, delimit, or forbid the assembling of believers. We have always supported the underground church in nations where Christian congregational worship is deemed illegal by the state.

When officials restrict church attendance to a certain number, they attempt to impose a restriction that *in principle* makes it impossible for the saints to gather *as the church*. When officials prohibit singing in worship services, they attempt to impose a restriction that *in principle* makes it impossible for the people of God to obey the commands of Ephesians 5:19 and Colossians 3:16. When officials mandate distancing, they attempt to impose a restriction that *in principle* makes it impossible to experience the close communion between believers that is commanded in Romans 16:16, 1 Corinthians 16:20, 2 Corinthians 13:12, and 1 Thessalonians 5:26. In all those spheres, we must submit to our Lord.

Although we in America may be unaccustomed to government intrusion into the church of our Lord Jesus Christ, this is by no means the first time in church history that Christians have had to deal with government overreach or hostile rulers. As a matter of fact, persecution of the church by government authorities has been the norm, not the exception, throughout church history. "Indeed," Scripture says, "all who desire to live godly in Christ Jesus will be persecuted" (2 Tim. 3:12). Historically, the two main persecutors have always been secular government and false religion. Most of Christianity's martyrs have died because they refused to obey such authorities. This is, after all, what Christ promised: "If they persecuted Me, they will also persecute you" (John 15:20). In the last of the beatitudes, He said, "Blessed are you when people insult you and persecute you, and falsely say all kinds of evil against you because of Me. Rejoice and be glad, for your reward in heaven is great; for in the same way they persecuted the prophets who were before you" (Matt. 5:11–12).

As government policy moves further away from biblical principles, and as legal and political pressures against the church intensify, we must recognize that the Lord may be using these pressures as means of purging to reveal the true church. Succumbing to governmental overreach may cause churches to remain closed indefinitely. How can the true church of Jesus Christ distinguish herself in such a hostile climate? There is only one way: bold allegiance to the Lord Jesus Christ.

Even where governments seem sympathetic to the church, Christian leaders have often needed to push back against aggressive state officials. In Calvin's Geneva, for example, church officials at times needed to fend off attempts by the city council to govern aspects of worship, church polity, and church discipline. The Church of England has never fully reformed, precisely because the British Crown and Parliament have always meddled in church affairs. In 1662, the Puritans were ejected from their pulpits because they refused to bow to government mandates regarding use of the Book of Common Prayer, the wearing of vestments, and other ceremonial aspects of state-regulated worship. The British Monarch still claims to be the supreme governor and titular head of the Anglican Church.

But again: *Christ is the one true head of His church,* and we intend to honor that vital truth in all our gatherings. For that preeminent reason, we cannot accept and will not bow to the intrusive restrictions government officials now want to impose on our congregation. We offer this response without rancor, and not out of hearts that are combative or rebellious (1 Tim. 2:1–8; 1 Pet. 2:13–17), but with a sobering awareness that we must answer to the Lord Jesus for the stewardship He has given to us as shepherds of His precious flock.

To government officials, we respectfully say with the apostles, "Whether it is right in the sight of God to give heed to you rather than to God, you be the judge" (Acts 4:19). And our unhesitating reply to that question is the same as the apostles': "We must obey God rather than men" (Acts 5:29).

Our prayer is that every faithful congregation will stand with us in obedience to our Lord as Christians have done through the centuries.

# Bibliography

J. P. Abel, *L'âge de Caïn* (Les Éditions Nouvelles, Paris, 1947).

*Actes du Congrès de Lausanne III, Politique et loi naturelle* (C.L.C., Paris, 1967).

Digby Anderson and Peter Mullen, eds., *Faking it: The Sentimentalisation of Modern Society* (The Social Affairs Unit, London, 1998).

Lancelot Andrewes, *An Exposition Upon the Ten Commandments* (Richard Cotes, London, 1642).

Rabbi Marvin S. Antelman, *To Eliminate the Opiate: An In-depth Study of Communist and Conspiratorial Group Efforts to Destroy Jews and Judaism,* two volumes (1974 and 2018).

Thomas Aquinas, *Selected Political Writings,* ed. A. P. d'Entrèves (Blackwells, Oxford, 1954).

H. X. Arquillière, *L'augustinisme politique: Essai sur la formation des théories politiques au Moyen-Age* (Vrin, Paris, 1972 [1934]).

Augustine, *City of God.*

R. Barilier, *Nouvelle Revue de Lausanne,* June 25, 1977.

Jacques Barzun, *The Culture We Deserve* (Wesleyan University Press, Middletown, 1989).

Georges Bernanos, *Français si vous saviez* (Gallimard, Paris, 1961).

Jean-Marc Berthoud, *Apologie pour la Loi de Dieu* (L'Âge d'Homme, Lausanne, 1996).
    *Des Actes de l'Église: Le christianisme en Suisse romande* (L'Âge d'Homme, Lausanne, 1993).
    *Les Dix Commandements lus par la Bible: Une Lumière divine pour notre temps: Le huitième commandement: Tu ne voleras pas: L'Économie, Le Vol et l'Ordre de la Création* (Messages, Lausanne, Lulu.com, 2019).
    *L'école et la famille contre l'utopie* (L'Âge d'Homme, Lausanne, 1997).
    *L'Alliance de Dieu à travers l'Écriture sainte: Une Théologie biblique* (L'Âge d'Homme, Lausanne, 2012).
    *L'Histoire Alliancielle de l'Église dans le Monde,* five volumes (Messages, Lausanne, Lulu.com, 2018-2020).
    *Une religion sans Dieu: Les Droits de l'Homme contre la Bible* (Messages, Lausanne, Lulu.com, 2018 [1993]).

Theodore Beza, *Du droit des magistrats sur leurs sujets, 1574* (Droz, Genève, 1970).

André Biéler, *La pensée économique et sociale de Calvin* (Georg, Geneva, 1961).

John Blanchard, *Does God Believe in Atheists?* (Evangelical Press, 2000).

Charles Bridges, *Proverbs* (Banner of Truth, 1968 [1846]).

Harold O. J. Brown, *The Sensate Culture: Western Civilization Between Chaos and Transformation* (Word Publishing, Dallas, 1996).

R. L. Bruckberger, *Dieu et la politique* (Plon, Paris, 1971).
    *Oui à la peine de mort* (Plon, Paris, 1985).

Michael J. Buckley, *At the Origins of Modern Atheism* (Yale University Press, 1987).

John Calvin, *Institution de la religion chrétienne* (Toulouse, 1888).

Nigel M. de S. Cameron, *The New Medicine: Life and Death After Hippocrates* (Crossway Books, Wheaton, Illinois, 1992).

R. K. Campbell, *Le foyer chrétien: Bibles et traités chrétiens* (Vevey, 1976).

R. Cardinne-Petit, *Les otages de la peur* (N.E.L., Paris, 1948).

Étienne Catta, *La doctrine politique et sociale du Cardinal Pie* (Nouvelles Éditions Latines, Paris, 1991 [1957]).

Gudrun Cavin, *Kaj Munk: dramaturge, prophète et martyr* (Geneva: Labor et Fides, 1945).

Henry Chavannes, *L'objection de conscience* (Cahiers de la Renaissance Vaudoise, Lausanne, 1961).

Larry Christenson, *La famille chrétienne: Foi et Victoire* (Lausanne, 1977).

Stephen B. Clark, *Man and Woman in Christ: An Examination of the Roles of Men and Women in Light of Scripture and the Social Sciences* (Servant Books, Michigan, 1980).

John W. Cooper, *Body, Soul and Life Everlasting: Biblical Anthropology and the Monism-Dualism Debate* (Regent College Publishing, Vancouver, 1995).

Curtis I. Crenshaw and Grover E. Gunn, *Dispensationalism, Today, Yesterday, and Tomorrow* (Footstool Publications, Memphis, Tennessee, 1985).

Michel Creuzet, *Les corps intermédiaires* (Édition des Cercles Saint-Joseph, Martigny, 1964).

Jean Daujat, *L'ordre social chrétien* (Beauchesne, Paris, 1970).

Bertrand de Jouvenel, *Du Pouvoir: Histoire naturelle de sa croissance*

(Les Éditions du Cheval Ailé, Genève, 1945).
*De la Souveraineté: À la recherche du bien politique* (Éditions Génin, Paris, 1955).

Frédéric de Rougemont, *The Individualists in Church and State,* trans. Colin Wright (Wordbridge, Aalten, 2018).

Augusto del Noce, *The Crisis of Modernity* (McGill-Queens University Press, Montreal, 2014).
*Il problema dell'ateisomo* (Il Mulino, Bologna, 1990).
*L'irreligion occidentale* (Fac, Paris, 1995).

Mohammed El Shakankiri, *La philosophie juridique de Jeremy Bentham* (Bibliothèque de Philosophie du Droit, L. J. D. J., Paris, 1970).

Jacques Ellul, *La technique ou l'enjeu du siècle* (Armand Colin, Paris, 1954).
*Contre les violents* (Centurion, Paris, 1972).

Cornelio Fabro, *Introduction à l'athéisme moderne* (Anne Sigier, Sillery, Québec, 1999).

Edward Feser and Joseph M. Bessette, *By Man Shall His Blood Be Shed: A Catholic Defense of Capital Punishment* (Ignatius Press, San Francisco, 2018).

John M. Frame, *Medical Ethics: Principles, Persons and Problems* (Presbyterian and Reformed, Philadelphia, 1988).

Hans W. Frei, *The Eclipse of the Biblical Narrative: A Study in Eighteenth and Nineteenth Century Hermeneutics* (Yale University Press, New Haven, 1974).

Roger Garaudy, *Parole d'Homme* (Laffont, Paris).

Agénor de Gasparin, *La famille, ses devoirs, ses joies et ses douleurs* (Michel Lévy Frères, Paris, 1869).

E. R. Geehan, ed., *Jerusalem & Athens: Critical Discussions on the*

*Philosophy and Apologetics of Cornelius Van Til* (Presbyterian and Reformed, Phillipsburg, 1993).

John H. Gerstner, *Wrongly Dividing the Word of Truth: A Critique of Dispensationalism* (Wolgemuth and Hyatt, Brentwood, Tennessee, 1991).

Sergiu Grossu, *Vania Moisseieff, le jeune martyr de Volontirovka* (Catacombes, Courbevoie, 1976).

Vladimir Guettée, *De la papauté* (L'Âge d'Homme, Lausanne, 1990).

T. R. Ingram, ed., *Essays on the Death Penalty* (St. Thomas Press, Houston, 1978).
*The Two Powers* (St. Thomas Press, Houston, 1959).

A. R. Kayayan, *Pénologie: Considérations chrétiennes sur la peine de mort* (Perspectives Réformées, Palos Heights, 1993).

E. and A. Kayayan, *Le chrétien dans la cité* (L'Âge d'Homme, Lausanne, 1995).

Douglas F. Kelly, *The Emergence of Liberty in the Modern World: The Influence of Calvin on Five Governments from the 16th Through 18th Centuries* (Presbyterian and Reformed, Philadelphia, 1992).

Alfred Kuen, "Le chrétien et la crise d'autorité" in *Ichthus,* N° 67 (April 1977).

Georges de Lagarde, *La naissance de l'esprit laïque au déclin du Moyen-Age,* five volumes (Nauwelaerts, Louvain, 1956-1963).

François Laplanche, *La Bible en France entre mythe et critique XVIe-XIXe siècles* (Albin Michel, 1994).

Hans K. LaRondelle, *The Israel of God in Prophecy: Principles of Prophetic Interpretation* (Andrews University Press, Berrien Springs, 1983).

J. Maarten, *Le village sur la montagne: Tableau de l'Église fidèle sous le règne nazi* (Geneva, 1940).

Philip Mauro, *The Gospel of the Kingdom with an Examination of Dispensationalism* (Reiner Publications, Swengel, 1974).
*The Hope of Israel: What is it?* (Reiner Publications, Swengel, Pennsylvania, 1970).

Pierre Marcel, *Face à la critique: Jésus et les apôtres: Esquisse d'une logique chrétienne* (Labor et Fides-Kerygma, Genève-Aix-en-Provence, 1986).

*Mémoire concernant la séparation des Églises et de l'État en Suisse* (May 1977).

Vincent P. Miceli, *The Gods of Atheism* (Roman Catholic Books, Harrison, New York, 1971).

H. Mitchell, *Les massacres de septembre 1944* (N.E.L., Paris, 1959).

Kaj Munk, *La Croix sur l'étendard: Paroles sous l'oppression* (Paris, 1945).

Gary North, *Crossed Fingers: How the Liberals Captured the Presbyterian Church* (Institute for Christian Economics, Tyler, 1996).
*Tactics of Christian Resistance* (Geneva Divinity School Press, Tyler, Texas, 1983).
*The Theology of Christian Resistance* (Geneva Divinity School Press, Tyler, Texas, 1983).

Francis Oakley, *Omnipotence, Covenant and Order: An Excursion in the History of Ideas from Abelard to Leibniz* (Cornell University Press, Ithaca, 1984).
*Politics and Eternity: Studies in the History of Medieval and Early-Modern Political Thought* (Brill, Leiden, 1999).

Jean-Marie Paul, *Dieu est mort en Allemagne: Des Lumières à Nietzsche* (Payot, Paris, 1994).

Franklin E. Payne, *Biblical Medical Ethics: The Christian and the Practice of Medicine* (Mott Media, Milford, Michigan, 1985).

Jean Paulhan, *Lettre ouverte aux directeurs de la Résistance* (Pauvert, Paris, 1968).

John Perkins, *Confessions of an Economic Hit Man* (Berrett-Koehler Publishers, 2004).
    *New Confessions of an Economic Hit Man* (Ebury Press, 2018).

Stephen C. Perks, *A Defense of the Christian State* (The Kuyper Foundation, Taunton, 1998).
    *The Nature, Government and Function of the Church: A Reassessment* (The Kuyper Foundation, Taunton, 1997).

John Piper and Wayne Grudem, eds., *Recovering Biblical Manhood and Womanhood: A Response to Evangelical Feminism* (Crossway Books, Illinois, 1991).

Maurice Porot, *L'enfant et les relations familiales* (P.U.F., Paris, 1970).

Henning Graf Reventlow, *The Authority of the Bible and the Rise of the Modern World* (SCM Press, London, 1984).

David Riesman, Nathan Glazer, and Reuel Denney, *The Lonely Crowd: A Study of the Changing American Character* (Yale University Press, 1950).
    *Individualism Reconsidered* (The Free Press, 1954).

Jean Romain, *La dérive émotionnelle: Essai sur une époque en désarroi* (L'Âge d'Homme, Lausanne, 1998).

Albert Roustit, *La prophétie musicale dans l'histoire de l'humanité: Après l'archéologie, la musique confirme la Bible* (Éditions Horvath, Roanne, 1970).

R. J. Rushdoony, *The Institutes of Biblical Law,* three volumes (Ross House Books, Vallecito, 1973-1999).

Joseph Siri, *Gethsemani: Réflexions sur le Mouvement Théologique Contemporain* (Tequi, Paris, 1981).
    "La Culture," Chapter VII, Jean-Marc Berthoud, *L'Histoire alliancielle de l'Église dans le Monde, volume V: Le combat présent: L'Église et le monde dans un univers devenu non doctrinal* (Messages Lausanne, Lulu.com, 2020).

Pitirim A. Sorokin, *The Crisis of our Age* (Oneworld, Oxford, 1992 [1941]).
    *The American Sex Revolution* (Peter Sargent, Boston, 1956).

Friedrich Julius Stahl, *Die Philosophy of the Rechts nach geschichtlicher Unsicht* (J. C. B. Mohr, Heidelberg, 1830-1837).

Hendrik G. Stoker, *Conscience: Phenomena and Theories* (University of Notre Dame Press, Notre Dame, 2018).

Dominique Tassot, *La Bible au risque de la science de Galilée au P. Lagrange* (F. X. de Guibert, Paris, 1997).

E. L. Hebden Taylor, *The Christian Philosophy of Law, Politics and the State* (The Craig Press, Nutley, 1969).
    *Economics, Money and Banking: Christian Principles* (The Craig Press, 1978).
    *The New Legality in the Light of the Christian Philosophy of Law* (Presbyterian and Reformed, Philadelphia, 1967).
    *The Reformational Understanding of Family and Marriage* (The Craig Press, 1970).
    *Reformation or Revolution: A Study of Modern Society in the Light of Reformational and Scriptural Pluralism* (The Craig Press, 1970).

Tertullian, "On Idolatry," in *The Ante-Nicene Fathers, Volume III, Latin Christianity: Its Founder Tertullian* (Eerdmans, Grand Rapids, 1976).

Walter Ullmann, *The Growth of Papal Government in the Middle Ages* (Methuen, London, 1955).

Jean Marie Vaissière, *Fondements de la cité* (Cercles canadiens de formation civique, Québec, 1963).

J. H. van den Berg, *The Changing Nature of Man: Introduction to a Historical Psychology* (Dell Publishing Co., New York, 1961).

Henry R. Van Til, *The Calvinist Concept of Culture* (Presbyterian and Reformed, Philadelphia, 1972).

Clémy Vautier, *Les théories relatives à la souveraineté et à la résistance chez l'auteur des "Vindiciae contra tyrannos" (1579)* (F. Roth, Lausanne, 1947).

Henry Babcock Veatch, *Intentional Logic: A Logic Based on Philosophical Realism* (Archon Books, 1970).
 *Two Logics: The Conflict Between Classical and Neo-Analytic Philosophy* (Editiones Scholasticae, Neuenkirchen, 2019).

Pierre Viret, *Exposition of the Ten Commandments,* two volumes, trans. R. A. Sheats (Psalm 78 Ministries, 2020).

Dietrich von Hildebrand, *Le cheval de Troie dans la cité de Dieu* (Beauchesne, Paris, 1971).
 *La vigne ravagée* (Éditions du Cèdre, Paris, 1974).

Benjamin B. Warfield, Robert L. Dabney, and Geoffrey Thomas, *Women Speaking in the Church: What does the Scripture Say?* (Solid Ground Christian Books, Birmingham, Alabama, 2014).

David F. Wells, *God in the Wasteland* (Eerdmans, Grand Rapids, 1994).
 *Losing our Virtue* (Eerdmans, Grand Rapids, 1998).
 *No Place for Truth* (Eerdmans, Grand Rapids, 1993).

John W. Whitehead, *Battlefield America: The War on the American People,* foreword by Ron Paul (SelectBooks, 2015).

Ralph M. Wiltgen, *Le Rhin se jette dans le Tibre* (Dominique Martin

Morin, Bouère, 1992).

Sheldon S. Wolin, *Democracy Incorporated: Managed Democracy and the Specter of Inverted Totalitarianism* (Princeton University Press, Princeton, 2008).

John C. H. Wu, *Fountain of Justice: A Study in the Natural Law* (Sheed and Ward, New York, 1955).

Cameron Wybrow, *The Bible, Baconianism, and Mastery over Nature: The Old Testament and its Modern Misreading* (Peter Lang, Bern, 1991).

Alexander Zinoviev, *Les hauteurs béantes d'Alexandre Zinoviev* (L'Âge d'Homme, Lausanne, 1977).

www.ingramcontent.com/pod-product-compliance
Lightning Source LLC
Chambersburg PA
CBHW020426220526
45464CB00002B/582